This book is dedicated to my mother, who taught me by her example about the fun of language; to Mario Pei, my childhood guide on many linguistic adventures; and to Ann.

—*Robert Magnan*

To Rick, for his unconditional love and support during this "wordy" project. And to my muse, my inspiration, my angel— thank you for believing in me.

—*Mary Lou Santovec*

We also dedicate this book to Mark Twain, who is credited with a line sure to delight anyone who has ever had trouble spelling: "It's a damn poor mind that can think of only one way to spell a word."

1001 Commonly Misspelled Words

What Your Spell Checker Won't Tell You

Robert Mangan & Mary Lou Santovec

MJF BOOKS
NEW YORK

Published by MJF Books
Fine Communications
322 Eighth Avenue
New York, NY 10001

1001 Commonly Misspelled Words
LC Control Number 2004113503
ISBN 1-56731-710-3

Copyright © 2000 The McGraw-Hill Companies, Inc.

This special edition published by MJF Books in arrangement with The McGraw-Hill Companies, Inc.

Manufactured in the United States of America on acid-free paper ∞

MJF Books and the MJF colophon are trademarks of Fine Creative Media, Inc.

QM   10   9   8   7   6   5   4   3   2   1

Using This Book

This book lists 1001 of the words that are the most difficult to spell. (Actually, there are many more than 1001 listed here, but "1001" makes a catchier title than "1378" or "1659" or whatever!)

And, unlike other lists of words, such as your dictionary, you don't need to be able to spell a word correctly to find it here. Take your best shot at spelling the word the way it sounds; you'll either find the word itself (if it's spelled like it sounds) or a phonetically spelled version of the word with the correct spelling next to it. We can't give all the possible misspellings, of course, but we hope to include enough to get you to the correct spellings of the words that give you trouble.

Many words end in "-tion" or "-sion," pronounced "shun," or "-tious" or "-cious," pronounced "shush." We usually don't put that end on those words that are spelled phonetically. Since this is a regular sound and ending on many words, we leave it alone, but the beginning of the word will include its phonetic spelling. For example, if you don't know how to spell "cancellation," you can find it under the spelling "canselation" and next to it you will find the correct spelling.

There are many words that start with the "k" sound, but the beginning letter is "c." If that's a word you're unsure of, check the "c" words first. There are also many words that start with "c" that sound like they start with the "s" sound. Check the "c" words first for those as well. Then, if you don't find them, check the "s" words. For example, phonetic spellings of the word "cynic" are found in both the "c" words as "cinic" and in the "s" words as "sinic." In both cases the correct spelling is next to them. For most words that start with letters other than c or s, the initial sound could not be spelled with any other letter, so you'll find them listed only under that letter.

For selected words throughout this book, we've included comments that give you information that we hope will make the word more memorable to you. Many of these comments have to do with word origins, which are interesting. We believe that the more you know about a word, the more likely you'll remember its spelling. Other comments provide mnemonic hints to help you learn and remember how to spell that word. Some of the suggestions for remembering correct spellings may make you laugh. That's OK with us. In fact, it's good, because you're more likely then to remember our suggestions.

Italics, Boldface, and Asterisks

In creating this book, we've used certain conventions.

◆ Every entry that's an *incorrect* spelling is in *italics* (and looks like this).

◆ Every entry that's a **correct** spelling is in **boldface** (and looks like this).

◆ If the correct spelling is followed by an asterisk (*), you'll find a comment under that entry.

We've tried to make this book as easy to use as possible, but also to include the most words in the fewest pages, so it's convenient to carry with you.

You'll also find that we've often grouped words in families, which should help you notice similarities and differences.

As you use this book, you may be surprised that we've included some words that you would have no trouble spelling. If so, then you should feel good, because other people have trouble with these words. But then, consider this: other people may be wondering why we've included the words that you're looking up. The moral of the story: we all have trouble spelling certain words, but our problems are not always with the same words.

We encourage you to carry this book around and to use it whenever you write. And we encourage you to have some fun learning about the usual and unusual ways in which English words developed. (By the way, we limit our discussion of English to the American variety; after all, that's what you use and there's no reason to confuse the situation with word spellings that are used in Canada and the United Kingdom.)

Good Reading

There are lots of books out there devoted to words. In putting together this guide, we consulted the following, which we recommend:

The American Heritage Dictionary (Houghton-Mifflin)

Webster's New Encyclopedic Dictionary (Black Dog & Leventhal Publishers)

Dictionary of Word Origins, Joseph T. Shipley (Littlefield, Adams & Co.)

Webster's New World Misspeller's Dictionary (Simon and Schuster)

Word Traps: A Dictionary of the 5,000 Most Confusing Sound-Alike, Look-Alike Words, Jordan L. Linfield and Joseph Krevisky (Collier Books)

Words of Science and the History Behind Them, Isaac Asimov (Houghton-Mifflin)

Words from the Myths, Isaac Asimov (Houghton-Mifflin)

Dictionary of Word and Phrase Origins, William and Mary Morris, three volumes (Harper and Row)

Death by Spelling: A Compendium of Tests, Super Tests, and Killer Bees, David Grambs (Harper and Row)

Word Mysteries and Histories: From Quiche to Humble Pie, Editors of American Heritage Dictionary (Houghton-Mifflin)

Word Origins and their Romantic Stories, Wilfred Funk (Bell Publishing)

Spelling Made Simple, Stephen V. Ross (Doubleday)

Where in the Word: Extraordinary Stories Behind 801 Ordinary Words, David Muschell (Prima Publishing)

They Have a Word for It: A Lighthearted Lexicon of Untranslatable Words and Phrases, Howard Rheingold (Jeremy P. Tarcher)

How to Improve Your Spelling and Vocabulary, Jessica Davidson (Franklin Watts)

Origins: A Short Etymological Dictionary of Modern English, Eric Partridge (Greenwich House)

Spelling 101: 101 Handy Rules and Simple Exercises Let You Be Letter-Perfect Every Time, Claudia Sorsby (St. Martin's)

Six Minutes a Day to Perfect Spelling, Harry Shefter (Simon and Schuster)

Correct Spelling Made Easy, Norman Lewis (Bantam, Doubleday, Dell Publishing)

A Concise Dictionary of New Words, B.A. Phythian and Richard Cox (NTC Publishing Group)

Dunces, Gourmands, & Petticoats: 1,300 Words Whose Meanings Have Changed Through the Ages, Adrian Room (NTC Publishing Group)

303 Dumb Spelling Misstakes ... and What You Can Do About Them, David Downing (NTC Publishing Group)

Introduction

1001 Commonly Misspelled Words ... Wise Words About the Why's of Words

Let's start with two basic facts.

- ◆ Fact 1. Spelling is the arrangement of letters. It's not an intelligence test.
- ◆ Fact 2. People will judge you by your spelling, regardless of Fact 1.

So what can you do? You can spend your life reminding people of Fact 1—or you can just accept Fact 2 and work at improving your spelling. Consider the odds: there are millions of people out there and only one of you....

No matter what your teachers and maybe even your parents may have told you, spelling is not easy. That's because English is a mess.

Our language is the result of more than 1000 years of linguistic promiscuity. Let's briefly review the history of English. (If you hate history, you can skip to the next section—but you'll miss some good stuff!)

A Little History

The history of English language begins in the fifth century, when three Germanic tribes came to the British Isles. Angles, Saxons, and Jutes crossed the North Sea from the Jutland peninsula (the area that is now Denmark and northern Germany). The people who were living in Britain spoke a Celtic language, but they were pushed out by the Germanic invaders into Wales, Scotland, and the region of Brittany in France. Their Celtic language was displaced by the language of the invaders. That language became known as English, after the Angles, who were from Engle and spoke a language called Englisc.

During the next few centuries, four regional dialects of English developed. We won't go into detail, because another significant historical event disrupted the evolution of those dialects. In the ninth century, the Vikings invaded Britain from Scandinavia. As a result, only one region remained as an independent kingdom, West Saxon. By the tenth century, the dialect of that region became the official language of Britain, which language historians call Old English.

At this time the vocabulary of Old English consisted of an Anglo-Saxon base with words from the Scandinavian languages of the invaders as well as from the Latin used by the Romans who had lived in the British Isles.

From Latin came words that would eventually develop into **street, kitchen, kettle, cup, cheese, wine**, and **candle**, for example. Norse contributed the words that would become **sky, egg, cake, skin, leg, window, husband, fellow, skill, anger, flat, odd, ugly, get, give, take, raise, call**, and **die**, and such pronouns as **they, their**, and **them**.

Nearly two centuries later, in 1066, William the Conqueror and the Norman army from France invaded England and defeated the English King Harold. That invasion brought big changes to English life, including the way they communicated. The Old French language used by the Normans became the language of the Royal Court and the ruling and business classes.

Over time, both the political situation and the language continued to evolve. By about 1200, England and France were no longer a single kingdom. The English were again using their own language at all levels, but because of years of French domination it now included many French words, including political terms such as **prince, duke, county, city, village**, and **justice** and food terms such as **mutton** and **beef**.

Language historians call the language at this point in its evolution Middle English. If you've ever tried to read the works of the poet Geoffrey Chaucer, who lived in the second half of the 1300s, you know that Middle English was quite different from modern English. And if you've never read any Chaucer, here's a sample from *Troylus and Criseyde*:

Ye knowe eek that in fourme of speche is chaunge
With-inne a thousand yeer, and wordes tho
That hadden prys now wonder nyce and straunge
Us thinketh hem, and yet thei spake hem so,
And spedde as wel in love as men now do.

Easy? In modern English, those lines read be something like "You know also that speech changes in form over a thousand years and words that then had value we now think them very foolish and strange, and yet they spoke that way and succeeded in love as well as we do now." So old Chaucer knew that love may be eternal but that language changes.

Middle English was very different from region to region, which meant that almost any word might be spelled "correctly" in several ways. There was no standard, no basis for distinguishing between correct and incorrect spellings. In that way, at least, life was truly easier!

Then, toward the end of the 1400s, came an invention that would revolutionize the evolution of English and every other language in the Western world—the printing press. The press was the main force in the standardization of language. As long as every document had to be written by hand, documents remained rare and were guarded most carefully. But when it became possible to crank out dozens and hundreds of copies of any document, writing spread widely. And that expansion of written communication tended to standardize English—as well as French and German and many other languages.

The printing press came to England in 1476. As books became cheaper, more people became literate. And, since London had the most publishing houses, the dialect spoken there became the standard throughout the country. For the first time, spelling and grammar became fixed and in 1604 the first English dictionary was published. That event marked the beginning of the end for freedom in spelling!

The printing press may have standardized spelling, but English kept developing and growing for centuries. However, we won't cover that history here, because it's time to move on to the present.

We've got a lot of time to cover, so we'll summarize four centuries in a paragraph. English continued to absorb words from other languages. From the languages of India, for example, we borrowed words such as **pundit, shampoo, turban, pajamas,** and **juggernaut.** From Finnish we got **sauna,** from Japanese we got **tycoon,** from the Aborigines in Australia we got **kangaroo** and **boomerang,** and from the Spanish who settled in the New World we got the words **mustang, canyon, ranch, stampede,** and **vigilante.** These lists could go on and on, but we promised only one paragraph.

The Problem with Being Rich ...

From this very brief history of the evolution of English, you can understand how our language is so very rich. Our ancestors borrowed words extensively from other languages—and sometimes had words imposed upon them. But there's a problem with a language so rich: the alphabet can't carry the load.

In English, we use just the basic Roman alphabet, with only occasional diacritics (those little marks used in Romance, Germanic, and Slavic languages to adapt the 26 letters of the alphabet). So our "spelling tools" are woefully inadequate to represent all the sounds of the English language.

Spelling problems also occur because writing tends to be conservative, less likely to change than pronunciation. For example, centuries ago, people pronounced the final "b" in "climb" and "thumb." Somewhere along the way they were no longer pronouncing that letter, but the spelling continued unchanged. The same is true of the "w" in "sword," the "l" in "half," and the "k" in "knife." People used to pronounce the sounds represented by these letters; over the years, the pronunciation evolved, but the spelling stayed the same.

That's a little about the history of our language. But history never stops; our language keeps changing.

A lot of that change is natural. But some changes have resulted from conscious efforts.

For example, in 1886 the American Philological Society listed some 3500 words for which it recommended simplified spellings. That list may have been a little too long to have much effect.

A more limited proposal came in 1898, when the following 12 spellings were recommended to replace traditional spellings: *tho* (though), *altho* (although), *thru* (through), *thruout* (throughout), *thoro* (thorough), *thoroly* (thoroughly), *thorofare* (thoroughfare), *program* (programme), *prolog* (prologue), *catalog* (catalogue), *pedagog* (pedagogue), and *decalog* (decalogue). Of this list, only two spellings—program and catalog—have become fairly standard.

In 1906 the Simplified Spelling Board recommended simplifying the spelling of 300 words. These changes found advocates, including President Theodore Roosevelt, who showed his support by ordering the United States Printing Office to adopt these spellings as standard in its documents. But changing the spelling of even only 300 words required too much effort and the initiative failed.

About 40 years later, the *Chicago Tribune* tried to promote spelling reform and used a number of simplified forms in its pages. But even an influential newspaper was unable to make a significant difference in the way we spell our language.

And the problem of spelling just keeps getting worse.

We're inundated with new words, particularly from the worlds of technology, medicine, and business. Of course, the younger generation, as always, is very creative, coming up with terms that keep the language alive—and confusing.

And because of the format in which these words are used and our lack of time, we usually don't have much opportunity to learn to spell all these words as we encounter them.

Because life keeps getting faster, we tend to have less time to read than our parents and grandparents—or at least we tend to read faster, to skim for information. As a result, we generally don't notice the spelling of all those words that we process.

The broadcast media exposes us to a lot of new words, which means that we hear and understand those words, but we don't see them written out, so it's harder to learn how to spell them correctly.

Of course, not all those words are new: sometimes the media folks—from news to sports—use words to impress us. They pepper their commentaries with such words as "phenomenal" and "perennial" and "melee" and "propitious" and ... the list goes on and on. We understand those words, and we may even be comfortable using them, but then, when we try to use them in writing, we may realize (or not) that we don't know how to spell them.

Logic?

In many languages, spelling is fairly logical. Every sound has one or, in rare cases, just a few ways to spell it. But it's not like that in English. As we mentioned earlier, English uses words taken from Anglo-Saxon, French, Latin, Greek, German, Spanish, Dutch, and other languages. So we use bits and pieces of the logic from other languages—and the results can be quite confusing. The correspondence between the sounds and the letters, between pronunciation and spelling, sometimes seems quite illogical.

Let's take an example. You know how to spell "fish." That's easy. It seems logical. But you could also spell the pronunciation of that little word as *ghoti*. That's right. Just take the *gh* from **tough**, the *o* from **women**, and the *ti* from **nation**. Pronounce all those letters and you'll have the word "fish"—*ghoti*. That's not the traditional spelling, of course, but those letters represent the sounds in that word.

That example may seem absurd—but only because you have no trouble spelling "fish." But just try to explain to a foreigner why the sounds "uf" and "oo" and "o" and "aw" and "ow" can all be spelled with the letters "ough"—as in the words **tough, through, though, thought**, and **bough**. Or try explaining why the spellings **kernel** and **colonel** represent a single pronunciation.

How about one more example? When you hear the "sh" sound, you have to choose among at least 17 ways to spell that sound, depending on the word in which it's used: **sh**ock, **s**ure, appre**c**iate, o**c**ean, ma**ch**ine, musta**ch**e, stan**ch**ion, fu**chs**ia, **sch**ist, con**sc**ious, nau**s**ea, exten**s**ion, pre**ss**ure, admi**ss**ion, ini**t**iate, atten**ti**on, and lu**x**ury.

As we said, in English the correspondence between the sounds and the letters can sometimes be very illogical. Even if you're familiar with the various languages that have contributed to our vocabulary, the outcome isn't always systematic.

Also, because of the borrowings from other languages and the natural development of the language, we have a lot of homophones—

words that sound the same but have different meanings and spellings, such as **to** and **too** and **two** or **sight** and **site** and **cite**.

Add to the confusion the fact that native speakers of English don't always agree on how to spell some words. So in the U.S. we have **color** and **defense** and **center**, to give just three examples, but in Canada and the United Kingdom they have *colour* and *defence* and *centre*.

As you can see, spelling in English is a tricky proposition. This book is designed to help you overcome the problems of American English spelling. We've identified the 1001+ words that you and many others are most likely to trip over, given you the phonetic spellings of these words, and provided some background and hints on how to remember how to spell many of them. We hope you enjoy using this book.

1001
Commonly
Misspelled
Words

Correct spelling	Incorrect spelling
	abarant → **aberrant**
	abaration → **aberration**
	abarigny → **aborigine**
	abberant → **aberrant**
	abberation → **aberration**
	abberigine, abberrigine → **aborigine**
	abbis → **abyss***
abbreviate, abbreviation	
	abbut, abbutt → **abut**
	abbys, abbyss → **abyss***
	abcess → **abscess**
	abdacate → **abdicate**
	abdamen → **abdomen**
abdicate	
abdomen	
abdominal	

Although it's **abdomen** with an −e, the adjective is **abdominal** with an −i.

	aberigine, aberiginy → **aborigine**
aberrant, aberration	
	aberrigine, aberriginy → **aborigine**
abhor, abhorrence	
	abis → **abyss***
	abizmul → **abysmal***

Correct spelling   *Incorrect spelling*

abominable
> This word comes from a Latin verb meaning "to deprecate as a bad omen," a root that also gives us **abomination**.

aborigine

abracadabra
> This word goes back to ancient Persian mythology. It was then appropriated by a Greek Christian cult. Then, in the Middle Ages it assumed magical powers. Now it's just a stock term used by magicians.

abreviate	**abbreviate**
abreviation	**abbreviation**
absalute	**absolute**
absalutely	**absolutely**

abscess

abscond

absence, absent, absentee, absenteeism, in absentia
> The word **absence** comes from a Latin verb meaning "to be away," related in origin to its antonym, **presence**.

absolute, absolutely

absorb, absorbent, absorbency, absorption

absurd, absurdity, absurdly

abundance, abundant

abut

abysm, abysmal, abyss
> The origin of these words is a Greek word for "bottomless."

academic, academically

acalade	**accolade**

a cappella (or a capella)
> This expression is Italian, meaning "in chapel style"—singing without instrumental accompaniment.

accademic	**academic**
accapella	**a cappella***

Correct spelling	*Incorrect spelling*

accelerate

This word comes from the Latin word that gives us **celerity** (speed). That may not help you remember how to spell **accelerate**, but it's an impressive word to add to your vocabulary.

accept/except

Accept means **receive**. **Except** means **exclude**. The greatest source of confusion is the expression, "present company excepted."

acceptable

accesery   **accessory**

access, accessible, accessibility

accessory, accessorize

accetylene   **acetylene**

accident, accidentally

The common pronunciation of **accidentally** makes this word more difficult to spell. Just think of **accidental** and the suffix *–ly*.

acclaim, acclamation

acclimate

accolade

accommodate, accommodation

Remember the double *c's* and double *m's* in these words.

accompany, accompaniment

accomplish, accomplishment

accord

accordion

It helps to think of the **accordion** keys as being in **accord**.

accountable, accountability

accouterment

This word comes from the French, with its origin in the verb meaning "to arrange or furnish."

accronim, accronym   **acronym***

accrual, accrue

accumen   **acumen***

Correct spelling	*Incorrect spelling*

accumulate, accumulation, accumulative
  The Latin root word, *cumulus,* meant "heap," a root we use in
  English for **cumulous** clouds.

accuracy, accurate

accuse, accusation, accusative, accusatory

accustom

acellerate	**accelerate***
aceptable, aceptible	**acceptable**
acesible	**accessible**
acessory	**accessory**

acetylene

ache

achieve, achievement
  Apply the principle, "i before e, except after c."

acident	**accident**

acknowledge, acknowledgment (or **acknowledgement**)

aclaim	**acclaim**
aclamate	**acclimate**

acme
  This word comes from the Greek, where it meant "highest point."
  Now most people become familiar with this word through the
  Roadrunner and Wily Coyote cartoons.

acnowledge	**acknowledge**
acolade	**accolade**
acomodate	**accommodate***
acompany	**accompany**
acompaniment	**accompaniment**
acomplish	**accomplish**
acord	**accord**
acordion	**accordion***
acoumen	**acumen***

Correct spelling	*Incorrect spelling*

acountability, acountibility	**accountability**
acountable, acountible	**accountable**
acoustic	
acoutrament	**accouterment***
acquaint, acquaintance	

acquiesce, acquiescence, acquiescent
The Latin root meant "to be at rest." We have the related words **quiescent** and **quiet**.

acquire, acquisition

acquit, acquitted, acquittal

acronym
This word is Greek in origin, from a word meaning "tip" or "top," as in **acrophobia** (fear of heights), and a word meaning "name," as in **pseudonym**. An **acronym** is a "name" formed from the "tips" of words.

acrophobia
This word comes from the Greek word for "top," which is found in the **Acropolis** and **acrobat**, and the Greek word for "fear."

across
This one is easy if you think of the words **a** and **cross** combined.

actionable

actual, actuality, actually

acumalate	**accumulate**
aculation	**accumulation**

acumen
This word comes from a Latin word for "sharp," as in **acute**.

acumulative	**accumulative**
acuracy, acurasy	**accuracy**
acurate	**accurate**
acusation	**accusation**
acusative	**accusative**

Correct spelling	*Incorrect spelling*

acusatory	**accusatory**
acuse	**accuse**
acustic	**acoustic**

acute, acuity
These words come from the Latin word for "sharp."

ad/add
Ad is short for **advertisement**. (In England, the short form is advert.) **Add** is to do **addition**.

adamant

adapt, adaptable, adaptation
Adapt is to modify, to make something **apt**. Don't confuse with **adopt**, which is to take, from the Latin word that also gives us **opt**.

adaquate	**adequate**
adaquatly	**adequately**

add/ad (see entry for **ad/add**)

addequate	**adequate**
addequately	**adequately**

addict, addiction, addictive
These words come from a Latin verb meaning "to sentence."

addolescent	**adolescent**

address, addressable

addultry	**adultery**

adequate, adequately
This word comes from two Latin words meaning "to make equal," as in **equate**.

adhere, adherent

adict	**addict***
adiction	**addiction**
adictive	**addictive**

adieu/ado
Adieu is French for "farewell." **Ado** means "fuss," now used chiefly in the expressions "much ado about nothing" and "without further ado ...."

Correct spelling	*Incorrect spelling*

adios

This word is Spanish for "goodbye," meaning "to God," as in the French **adieu**. It's similar to goodbye—originally "God be with you."

adiquit   **adequate**

adjudicate, adjudication, adjudicator

The root of these words is Latin, meaning "to judge."

adjunct

admission, admit, admittance

admonish, admonition

ad nauseam

We borrowed this expression directly from Latin, meaning "to the point of nausea," so spell it with **nausea**. The Latin word came from Greek, where it derived from *naus*, the word for ship, logically, a root that also developed into such words as **nautical** and (much later) **astronaut**.

ado/adieu (see entry for **adieu/ado**)

adolescent, adolescence

adress   **address**

adressable, adressible   **addressable**

adulation

adultery, adulterous, adulterer

advantage, advantageous

adverse

This word, meaning "unfavorable" or "harmful," comes from a Latin word meaning "to turn toward or against." Don't confuse with **averse**, meaning "feeling distaste or repugnance," from a similar but opposite Latin word meaning "to turn away."

advertise, advertisement

Advertise is one of 11 commonly misspelled verbs ending in –*ise*. The others are **apprise**, **advise**, **chastise**, **despise**, **devise**, **exercise**, **improvise**, **revise**, **supervise**, and **surprise**.

advice/advise

These quasi homophones are sometimes confusing. **Advice** is opinions or suggestions. **Advise** is to offer opinions or suggestions.

| Correct spelling | *Incorrect spelling* |

advise/advice (see entry for **advice/advise**)

advise, advisor/adviser, advisable, advisory
Even the experts can't decide between adviser and advisor: both spellings are acceptable.

aerobic
This word for exercises that get us breathing heavily comes from the Greek word for "air," *aer-*, which we find in such words as **aerial** and **aerodynamic**.

aerodinamic   **aerodynamic**

aerodynamic

aerosol
This modern creation comes from the Greek word for "air" and the Latin-based **solution**.

aesthetic, aesthetics or **esthetic, esthetics**
The spelling of these words is still changing. They came into English from German, from a Greek word, *aistheta* ("perceptible things").

afadavit   **affidavit***

afect   **affect***/**effect**

afection   **affection**

afectionate   **affectionate**

affect
This is a verb meaning "to act on, to influence." Don't confuse with **effect**, which can also be a verb, meaning "to cause or bring about," but which is generally a noun, meaning "result." **Affect** is also a noun used by psychologists to mean "feeling or emotion."

affection, affectionate

affidavit
This legal term comes from the Middle Ages, from the Latin verb, *affidare*, which meant "to pledge."

affiliate, affiliated, affiliation
The Latin root of these words is *affiliare*, meaning "to adopt," hence our use for indicating a created relationship.

affinity
afflict, afflicted, affliction
affluence, affluent
affront

Incorrect spelling	Correct spelling
afidavit	**affidavit***
afiliate	**affiliate***
afiliated	**affiliated***
afiliation	**affiliation***
afinity	**affinity**
afluance	**affluence**
afluant	**affluent**
afrodisiac	**aphrodisiac**
afront	**affront**

against
aggravate, aggravated
> These words come from the Latin word that gives us **grave**, meaning "serious." To **aggravate** is to make a situation more serious.

aggregate
aggressive, aggression
agnostic
> This word comes from two Greek words meaning "not know." The second root word is also found in **diagnosis** ("distinguishing, knowing apart"), **prognosis** ("knowing in advance"), and **prognosticate** ("to know in advance, to predict").

agoraphobe, agoraphobia, agoraphobic
> These words come from the Greek words for "marketplace" and "fear," to mean a fear of being in open spaces.

agrarian

Incorrect spelling	Correct spelling
agravate	**aggravate**
agregate	**aggregate**
agresive	**aggressive**

Correct spelling	*Incorrect spelling*

Incorrect spelling	Correct spelling
aile	**aisle***
airagance	**arrogance**
airagant	**arrogant**
airobic	**aerobic***
airodynamic	**aerodynamic**
airogance	**arrogance**
airogant	**arrogant**
airosol	**aerosol***

aisle/isle
   An **aisle** is a passageway. An **isle** is an island.

Incorrect spelling	Correct spelling
akademik	**academic**
akalade	**accolade**
akapella	**a cappella***
akclimate	**acclimate**
ake	**ache**

akin

Incorrect spelling	Correct spelling
aklame	**acclaim**
akme	**acme***
aknowledge	**acknowledge**
akomadate	**accommodate***
akompany	**accompany**
akompanyment	**accompaniment**
akord	**accord**
akrofobia	**acrophobia***
akronim	**acronym***
akross	**across***
akrual, akrue	**accrual, accrue**
akselerate	**accelerate***
aksept	**accept**
aksesory	**accessory**

Correct spelling	*Incorrect spelling*

aksess	**access**
akshul	**actual**
aksident	**accident***
aksiom	**axiom**
akumen	**acumen***
akumulate	**accumulate**
akuracy	**accuracy**
akurate	**accurate**
akuse, akkuse	**accuse**
akustik	**acoustic**
akustom	**accustom**
akute	**acute***
akuterment	**accouterment***
akwies	**acquiesce**
akwire	**acquire**
akwit	**acquit**

alacrity

albatross

It's believed that this word came from the Spanish and Portuguese words for "pelican"—*alcatraz*, as in the notorious prison island in San Francisco Bay. (The word was originally Arabic for "water carrier," but the initial *alca* changed to *alba*, Latin for "white," which seemed more logical.) Now this large seabird represents a burden or bad luck.

albeit

When you use this word, you're using a Middle English contraction for "although it be."

albetross	**albatross***

alchemy

aledge, alege	**allege**
alegator	**alligator***

Correct spelling	*Incorrect spelling*

alein, aleinate	**alien, alienate**
alergy	**allergy**
aleviate	**alleviate***

algebra
This word came into Middle English through medieval Latin from an Arabic word, *al-jebr*—"the (science of) reuniting." When the word was borrowed, the definite article *al* became part of the noun.

algorithm
This word for a mechanical or recursive computational procedure came into Middle English from the name of an Arabic mathematician and author of a treatise on mathematics, Muhammad ibn-Musa Al-Kharzimi or Al-Khwarizimi.

alien, alienate

aligator	**alligator***
allacrity	**alacrity**
allbeit	**albeit***

allegation, allege, alleged, allegedly

allegiance

allein	**alien**
alleinate	**alienate**

allergy

alleviate, alleviated
These words come from the Latin word that gives us *levity*. To alleviate is to make a situation lighter, less serious.

allien	**alien**
allienate	**alienate**

alligator
We borrowed this word from the Spanish, *el lagarto*—"the lizard." In the borrowing, the definite article *el* became part of the noun.

allot/a lot
Allot is a verb meaning "to distribute by lot" or "to allocate."
A lot means "many."

Correct spelling	*Incorrect spelling*

allotted

allowed/aloud

Allowed is synonymous with "permitted." **Aloud** is the opposite of "quietly."

all ready/already

All ready means "completely prepared." **Already** means "by now or by any specified time."

all right

This expression is generally spelled as two words.

all together/altogether

All together is used with a number of items that are considered collectively. **Altogether** means "completely" or "on the whole."

allude/elude

These two quasi homophones are similar in formation but quite different in use. To **allude** is to make an indirect reference. To **elude** is to evade, avoid, or escape.

allurgy   **allergy**

allusion/illusion

Allusion is an implied or indirect reference. **Illusion** is a misleading appearance or image.

all ways/always

All ways means "in every manner." **Always** means "every time" or "continuously" or "forever."

almost

aloha

This word is Hawaiian for "love," used as a greeting or farewell.

aloof

alot   **a lot/allot**

a lot/allot (see entry for **allot/a lot**)

aloud/allowed (see entry for **allowed/aloud**)

already/all ready (see entry for **all ready/already**)

altar/alter

Altar is a structure used for worship. **Alter** as a verb means "to modify" and as an adjective means "other" (**alter ego**—"other self").

Correct spelling   *Incorrect spelling*

alter/altar (see entry for **altar/alter**)

alterior   **ulterior**

alternative

although

altogether/all together (see entry for **all together/
    altogether**)

altruistic

alude   **allude**

alumna, alumnae, alumni, alumnus
> These words are straight Latin, marked for gender and number:
> *−a* for feminine singular, *−us* for masculine singular, *−ae* for femi-
> nine plural, and *−i* for masculine or mixed plural.

alurgy   **allergy**

alusion   **allusion/illusion***

always/all ways (see entry for **all ways/always**)

amalgamation

amateur
> The *−eur* ending reveals the French origin of this word. The ending
> denotes somebody who does something; in this case, it's somebody
> who loves doing something, who doesn't do it for compensation.

ambassador
> Note that the **ambassador** with an *a-* works in an **embassy**
> with an *e-*.

ambidextrous
> The Latin root for this word shows a persistent cultural bias
> against left-handed people: it consists of *ambi*, "both," and *dextera*,
> "right hand."

ambience, ambient
> This word is almost pure Latin, from *ambiens*, "going around."

ambiguity, ambiguous

ameliorate

amenable

Correct spelling   *Incorrect spelling*

amend/emend

Amend means "to improve." **Emend** has the same meaning, only more specific, generally used only for improving a text.

amenity, amenities

ammateur	**amateur***
ammenable	**amenable**
ammend	**amend**
ammenities	**amenities**
ammenity	**amenity**
ammortize	**amortize***
ammoung	**among***
ammount	**amount**

ammunition

among

The variant **amongst** is chiefly literary.

amortize

This word comes from a Middle French word for "to deaden," derived from a Latin term meaning "to death."

amount

amphetamine

amunition	**ammunition**

anachronism, anachronistic

These words derive from the Greek, *ana-* (backwards) and *chronos* (time), as found in such words as **chronology**, **chronicles**, and **chronometer**.

anaerobic

This word for microorganisms that can live without the presence of free oxygen comes from the Greek word for "air," *aer-*, which we find in such words as **aerial** and **aerodynamic**.

anahistamine	**antihistamine**

analog, analogous, analogy

analysis, analyst, analytical, analyze

Only two common verbs in English end in *–yze*: **analyze** and **paralyze**.

Correct spelling	*Incorrect spelling*

ananimity	**anonymity**
ananimous	**anonymous**

anarchy, anarchism, anarchist

Anartic	**Antarctic**

Just remember that this piece of land and ice forms an *arc* over the southern polar region.

anasedent	**antecedent**
anasthesia	**anesthesia***
anasthesiologist	**anesthesiologist***

anathema

This Greek word originally meant "an accursed thing." The meaning weakened over the centuries to now mean "denunciation" or simply to refer to something disliked intensely.

anaversary	**anniversary***

ancient

andragogy

This word is a very recent creation, from Greek words meaning "male" or "man" and "to lead (or educate)." It's a sexist term for adult education, based on the term **pedagogy**, "education (of children)."

androgynous, androgyny

anecdote

This word for a little story comes from a Greek word meaning "unpublished." Don't confuse with **antidote**, also from the Greek, meaning "something given against (the effects of a poison)."

anesthesia, anesthesiologist, anesthesiology

The root of these words is Greek, *anaisthesia*, meaning "insensibility." An older spelling with *–ae-* is still used occasionally: **anaesthesia**, **anaesthesiologist**, and **anaesthesiology**.

aneurism, anurism, anurysm	**aneurysm**
aneversary	**anniversary***

angel/angle

Angel is a heavenly or spiritual being. **Angle**, as a noun, is a cor-

Correct spelling	*Incorrect spelling*

ner or an approach and, as a verb, means to fish or (from a figurative extension) to seek something subtly. These are not true homophones, but they're sometimes confused in spelling.

angelic

angle/angel (see entry for **angel/angle**)

anialate	**annihilate**
anihistamine, anihistimine	**antihistamine**
aniversary, aniversery, annaversary	**anniversary***

annihilate

anniversary
This word comes from two Latin words, for "year" and "(re)turn," for something that returns every year. (The term became the French word for "birthday," another event that returns every year.)

annoint	**anoint**

annotate

annual, annually

annul, annulled, annulling, annulment
This verb comes through Old French from the Latin combination of *ad* (to) and *nullus* (none), the second word also making it into English as **null** and **nullify**.

anoint

anomaly

anonymity, anonymous
The Greek root of these words means "without a name." We find part of this root in such words as **antonym**, **synonym**, and **pseudonym**.

anorexia, anorexic
The Greek root of these words means "without appetite."

anotate	**annotate**

answer

antagonism, antagonist, antagonistic
These words derive from a Greek verb meaning "to struggle

Correct spelling	*Incorrect spelling*

against," from *anti-* (against) and *agon* (contest), the second part coming into English in such words as **agonize** and **agony**, in addition to **protagonist**.

antalope	**antelope**
antanym	**antonym**

In this word it's easy to recognize the Greek roots—*anti-* (against) and *onyma* (name), a root that we also find in **synonym, pseudonym**, and **anonymous**.

Antarctic

This comes from *ant-* (against) and *Arctic*, thus the area opposite the North Pole—the South Pole.

antebellum

antecede

There are only seven verbs in English that end in *–cede*. In addition to **antecede**, we have **cede, concede, intercede, precede, recede,** and **secede**.

antecedent

The prefix *ante-* is Latin for "before." Don't confuse it with the Greek *anti-*, which means "against." The *–cede-* means "to move." So an **antecedent** is something that goes before something else. This word is related to **ancestor**.

anteclimactic	**anticlimactic**
anteclimax	**anticlimax**

antediluvian

This fancy synonym for "ancient" derives from two Latin words: *ante* (before)—as in **antebellum, antecedent**—and *diluvium* (flood)—as in **diluvial** and (through Old French) **deluge**.

antedote	**antidote***

antelope

antenym	**antonym***

anthracite

anthropomorphic, anthropomorphism

Correct spelling	*Incorrect spelling*

antibellum	**antebellum**
anticapate	**anticipate**
anticedent	**antecedent***
anticipate, anticipatory	
anticlimactic, anticlimax	
antics	
antidiluvian	**antediluvian***

antidote

    This word comes from a Greek word meaning "something given against (the effects of a poison)." Don't confuse with **anecdote**, from the Greek for "unpublished," now meaning a little story.

antihistamine

antipathy

antiquated, antique

antisedent	**antecedent***

antithesis, antithetical

antonym

anual	**annual**
anul, anull	**annul***

anxiety, anxious

aparant	**apparent**
aparantly	**apparently**
aparatis, aparatus	**apparatus**
aparent	**apparent**
aparently	**apparently**

apartheid

    This word is a rare borrowing from Afrikaans, of French origin, meaning "separateness, the state of being apart."

apartment

    It's easy to spell this word if you think of each unit as standing **apart**, separate from the others.

Correct spelling   *Incorrect spelling*

apathetic, apathy

apatiser	**appetizer**
apatite	**appetite**
apatizer	**appetizer**
apend	**append**
apendage	**appendage***
apendectomy	**appendectomy**
apendicitis	**appendicitis**
apendix	**appendix**
apetiser	**appetizer**
apetite	**appetite**
apetizer	**appetizer**
aplacation	**application**
apliance	**appliance***
aplicable	**applicable**
aplication	**application**
aplience	**appliance***

apocalypse, apocalyptic

apocryphal

apointment	**appointment**

apologetic, apology

apoplectic, apoplexy

apossum	**opossum***

apostrophe

apparatus

apparent, apparently

appartheid, apparthied	**apartheid***
appartment	**apartment***
appatiser	**appetizer**
appatite	**appetite**

| **Correct spelling** | *Incorrect spelling* |

appatizer	**appetizer**

appear, appearance

append, appendage
We use **append** to mean "to attach," but the Latin root, *appendere*, means "to hang upon."

appendectomy, appendicitis, appendix
The plural is either **appendixes** or (usually in scholarly or scientific texts) **appendices**.

appetiser	**appetizer**

appetite

appetizer, appetizing

applacable	**applicable**
applacation	**application**

appliance
This word was created from the verb **apply**, for a machine applied to a certain household need.

applicable, application

applience	**appliance**

apply, applies, applying

appocalyptic	**apocalyptic**
appocriphal, appocryphal	**apocryphal**

appoint, appointment

appology	**apology**
appoplexy	**apoplexy**

appraisal, appraise
These words come from the Latin word that gives us **price** and the closely related **appreciate**. Don't confuse with **apprise**, which means "to notify or inform."

appreciate, appreciation

apprehend, apprehension

apprise
Apprise is one of 11 commonly misspelled verbs ending in *–ise*. The

others are **advertise, advise, chastise, despise, devise, exercise, improvise, revise, supervise,** and **surprise**.

appropos   **apropos**

Although **apropos** often means **appropriate**, the former comes from the French words *à propos*, meaning "on the subject," and the latter goes back to the Latin words *ad proprius*, which became *appropriare*, to make one's own.

appropriate

approximate, approximately

apraise	**appraise**
apreciate	**appreciate**
aprehend	**apprehend**
aprise, aprize	**apprise**

apropos

apropriate	**appropriate**
aproximate	**approximate**
apserd	**absurd**
apserdity	**absurdity**
apserdly	**absurdly**

apt

aptitude

aquaint	**acquaint**

aqueous

aquiese	**acquiesce***
aquire	**acquire**
aquit	**acquit**
aragance	**arrogance**
aragant	**arrogant**
arange	**arrange**

arbitrarily, arbitrary

arcaic	**archaic***

Correct spelling	*Incorrect spelling*

arcane

archaic

This word came into English through French from the Greek word for "old-fashioned," from the root *arkhe*, meaning "beginning." Anything that goes back to the beginning is truly **archaic**.

Arctic

ardent

arguable, arguably, argue, arguing, argument

These words came from the Latin, *arguere*, meaning "to make clear"—something that most arguments fail to do!

aristocracy, aristocrat

Government by nobility dates back to the Greeks. **Aristocracy** comes from *aristos*, meaning "best," and *kratia*, meaning "power" or "rule." We now prefer **democracy**, power to the people (*demos*).

arithmetic

The root of this word is *arithmos*, Greek for "number" (quite logically).

Armageddon

arobic	**aerobic***
arodynamic	**aerodynamic**
arogance	**arrogance**
arogant	**arrogant**
arosol	**aerosol***

around

arpeggio

This musical term for notes in a chord played successively comes from an Italian verb, *arpeggiare*, meaning "to play the harp," from a word of Germanic origin, *arpa* (harp). (Our word **harp** came by way of Old French, where it gained the initial *h*.)

arragance	**arrogance**
arragant	**arrogant**

arrange, arrangement

Correct spelling	*Incorrect spelling*

arrogance, arrogant

artefact

This spelling is accepted, but **artifact** is preferred.

Artic   **Arctic***

article

articulate

artifact

This is the preferred spelling of this word, although **artefact** is an accepted variant.

asailant	**assailant**
asalt	**assault**
asassin	**assassin***
asassinate	**assassinate***
asassination	**assassination***
asault	**assault**

ascend, ascendance, ascendant, ascent

ascertain

This spelling is easy, since the word means to discover something *as certain*.

asend	**ascend**
asertain	**ascertain***
asetiline	**acetylene**
asfault	**asphalt**
asiduous	**assiduous***

asinine

This word causes problems because it comes directly from Latin, *asinus* (ass), rather than from the English **ass**.

asist	**assist**
asistance	**assistance**
asistant	**assistant**
asistence	**assistance**

Correct spelling   *Incorrect spelling*

Correct spelling	Incorrect spelling
asistent	**assistant**
asma	**asthma**
asociate	**associate**
asociation	**association**
asorted	**assorted**
asortment	**assortment**
asparagus	
asparin	**aspirin**
as per	
aspergus	**asparagus**
asperin	**aspirin**
asphalt	
asphault	**asphalt**
aspirin	
assailant	
assalt	**assault**
assanine	**asinine***

assassin, assassinate, assassination

These words come from an Arabic word meaning "hashish user." That was the name given to members of a secret society in Persia in the 11th century. Members of this sect, under the influence of the drug, would attack Christian leaders.

assault

assertain	**ascertain***
asset	
assfault	**asphalt**

assiduous

It was easier to be **assiduous** two millennia ago: the Latin root for this word was a verb, *assidere*, meaning "to sit near to," implying attention but not necessarily any effort.

assinine	**asinine***

Correct spelling	*Incorrect spelling*

assist, assistance, assistant

associate, association

assorted, assortment

assphalt   **asphalt**

assume, assumption
> Perhaps the best way to remember the spelling of **assume** is
> with the reminder that "when you **assume**, you make an **ass** out
> of **u** (you) and **me**."

assurance, assure

asterisk
> This word comes from Latin and Greek, meaning "little star," using
> the root that we find in **asteroid** and **disaster**.

asthma

astigmatism

astonish

astute

asume   **assume***

asumption   **assumption***

asynchronous

ataché   **attaché***

atack   **attack**

ate/eight
> The first of these homophones is the past tense of the verb "to eat"
> and the second is the number between seven and nine.

atempt   **attempt**

atend   **attend***

atendant   **attendant***

atenuate   **attenuate**

atheist

athlete, athletic, athletics
> Because of the difficulty of pronouncing –*thl*-, some people insert a
> vowel, which makes this word easier to pronounce and harder to spell.

Correct spelling	*Incorrect spelling*

atittude   **attitude**

atone

It's easy to spell this word if you remember that when you **atone** for an offense, you can become *at one* with the person offended.

atorney   **attorney**

atrium

attaché

This word is pure French, the title of a person officially assigned ("attached") to the staff of a diplomatic mission, but we usually use the word for a briefcase such as an **attaché** might carry.

attack

attempt

attendance, attendant, attendee

This third word is a recent, unfortunate creation; since the ending —ee denotes the recipient of an action, an **attendee** would be somebody who is attended, not somebody who attends.

attenuate

attitude, attitudinal

attone   **atone***

attorney

attrium   **atrium**

attune

atypical

audacious, audacity

audience

au jus

This expression is pure French, meaning "in the juice or gravy."

aukzilary   **auxiliary**

aulternative, aulternetive   **alternative**

aultruistic   **altruistic**

aural/oral

These two words are confused by many people because they're

Correct spelling	*Incorrect spelling*

both used in similar contexts. **Aural** means "pertaining to the ear." **Oral** means "pertaining to the mouth."

au revoir

This expression is pure French, for "goodbye" (literally, "until the seeing again").

ausome	**awesome**

auspicious

We tend to use this word only in the expression "**auspicious** occasion." That's a shame, because it's a good word, from *avis* (bird) and *spex* (watcher). But when the Romans watched birds, they did so not for fun but in order to predict the future.

austere, austerity

autamatic	**automatic**

authentic, authenticity

autherize	**authorize**

author, authorial, authoritative, authority

The word **author** had a stronger meaning in Latin, coming from a verb meaning "to create." That origin gave this word **authority** that it rarely has in our use.

authorize

autism, autistic

automatic

autumn, autumnal

auxiliary

avail, available

These words come from a Middle English verb, *availen*, borrowed from an Old French verb derived from a Latin verb meaning "to be worth."

avant-garde

This word comes directly from the French. The same word was also borrowed into English many centuries ago, to give us **vanguard**.

Correct spelling	*Incorrect spelling*

avarice, avaricious
These words come through Middle English from Old French with their origins in the Latin *avaritia*, from the verb *aver*, which simply meant "to desire." The same verb was the root of our **avid** and **avidity**.

avuncular

avvarice	**avarice***
avvaricious	**avaricious***
awdacious	**audacious**
awdacity	**audacity**

awe

aweful, awefull, awfull	**awful**

awesome
awful
awkward

awsome	**awesome**
awthur	**author***

axiom, axiomatic

axselerate	**accelerate***

bachelor

This word came into Middle English from Old French, where it meant "squire," a young noble who attended a knight (the term **squire** derived from a word meaning "shield-bearer") and prepared to become a knight.

bailiwick

This old English word for "jurisdiction" is related to **bail**, which you may need if you break any law in a **bailiwick**.

balance

balistic	**ballistic***
baliwick	**bailiwick***
ballance, ballence	**balance**

ballistic

This word is easy to spell if you remember that the word pertains to projectiles—and a very common projectile is a **ball**.

bamboozle

banal

banana

bandanna

To spell this word, just think of this apparel as the **band Anna** wears.

bane

This word goes back to Old English, where *bana* meant "murderer" or "destroyer." The meaning is figurative now and much milder, as we call someone or something "the bane of my existence" if it's just inconvenient or annoying.

Correct spelling   *Incorrect spelling*

---

bankrupt, bankruptcy

bannana, bannanna **banana**

baptism, baptize
These terms derive from the Greek, from the verb *bapzein,* which meant "to dip."

baracade **barricade**

baracuda **barracuda**

baral **barrel**

barbiturate

bare/bear
Bare means "naked" or "to make naked." **Bear** is an animal or a verb meaning "to carry." So you **bare** your soul, but you **bear** your burdens.

barel **barrel**

bargain

baricade, barikade **barricade**

barier **barrier**

bario **barrio***

barle **barrel**

barley

barracade **barricade**

barracuda

barrel

barricade

barrier

barrio
This word is Spanish for a predominantly Spanish-speaking neighborhood or enclave.

barrle **barrel**

bastion

batalion, batallion **battalion**

| **Correct spelling** | *Incorrect spelling* |

---

batchaler, batchalor, batcheler, batchelor	**bachelor***
batery	**battery**

battalion

battery

bazaar

This unusual spelling, with a single *a* and a double *a*, seems appropriate for this word from the Persian for an exotic marketplace consisting of stalls selling various items. Don't confuse this word with **bizarre,** which means "weird."

beach/beech

If you confuse these two words, just keep this in mind: **beach** is land by the *sea* and **beech** is a tree.

bear/bare (see entry for **bare/bear**)

beech/beach (see entry for **beach/beech**)

beginning

This word follows the rule for adding *–ing* to verbs: when the final syllable contains a short vowel, double the consonant and add *–ing*.

belicose, belikose	**bellicose**

belief, believable, believe

Here's a fun one: at the center of **believe** and **belief** is **lie.** Hmmm....

beligerence	**belligerence***
beligerent	**belligerent***

bellicose

belligerence, belligerent

These words come from two Latin words that mean "waging war." That Latin word for "war," *bellum*, is also found in such words as **antebellum** and **bellicose.**

benafactor	**benefactor**
benaficial	**beneficial***
benaficiary	**beneficiary***

Correct spelling	*Incorrect spelling*

benafit	**benefit***
benafitted	**benefited***

benefactor

beneficial, beneficiary
These words derive from Latin, *bene facere*, "to do good."

benefit, benefited
For the past tense or past participle, the spelling **benefitted** is also accepted.

benevolence, benevolent
These words derive from Latin, *bene volens*, "wishing good."
They're antonyms of **malevolence** and **malevolent**

benifactor	**benefactor**
benificial	**beneficial***
benificiary	**beneficiary***
benifit	**benefit***
benifited	**benefited***

benign, benignant

bennefactor	**benefactor**
benneficial	**beneficial***
benneficiary	**beneficiary***
bennefit	**benefit**
bennevolence	**benevolence***
bennevolent	**benevolent***

besmirch

beverage
This word came into Middle English from Old French from the Latin, *biber*, a root that we also find in **imbibe** and (perhaps) in **bib**.

biannual/biennial
These two words, although similar in form and origin, differ considerably in meaning. **Biannual** means "twice a year." **Biennial** means occurring every other year or lasting for two years.

bicentennial

Correct spelling	*Incorrect spelling*

biennial/biannual (see entry for **biannual/biennial**)

bigamist, bigamy

This word is a development from the Latin prefix *bi-*, meaning two, as in **binary** and **bicycle**, and the Greek root, *gamos*, meaning "marriage," as in **monogamy**.

Incorrect spelling	Correct spelling
bilding	**building**
biligerent	**belligerent***
bilionaire	**billionaire**
billigerent	**belligerent***

billionaire

biodegradable

biscuit

This is a French word, from medieval Latin, *biscoctus*, meaning "twice cooked." But what's a **biscuit**? That depends on which side of the Atlantic the word is used!

bisect

This word confuses some people, because they assume that since **dissect** has two *s*'s, **bisect** should work the same way. But the difference in spelling derives from the prefixes: it's *dis-* (apart) but *bi-* (in two).

Incorrect spelling	Correct spelling
biskit	**biscuit***

bite/byte

A **bite** is a small piece, such as in the recent creation, "sound bite." A **byte** is a computer term for a sequence of **bits** (digits 0 and 1 used in binary notation).

bituminous

bizarre

This word means "weird." Don't confuse it with **bazaar**, a shopping area or a type of sale.

Incorrect spelling	Correct spelling
bizness	**business**

blatant

bludgeon

blustery

Correct spelling	*Incorrect spelling*

bogus

bombast, bombastic

bona fide
This term is pure Latin, "in good faith" (and it's two words).

bonanza
This word is Spanish for "fair weather."

bookkeeper
This word may look odd, but it's a logical formation: **book** and **keeper**. It's one of the few English words with three double letters in a row.

botom, botum   **bottom**

bouillabaisse
This word and the highly seasoned seafood stew come to us from southern France. The word is a combination of the dialectal verbs "to boil" and "to lower."

boulevard

boundaries

bourgeois, bourgeoisie
These words denoting "middle class" come from the Old French word for "town," which in Late Latin meant "fortified place," with its roots in Germanic.

bottom

bouillon/bullion
Bouillon is a clear broth or a dehydrated solution used in cooking. **Bullion** is gold or silver in bars or ingots.

boyant, boyent   **buoyant**
It's easier to spell this word if you forget the pronunciation and just remember that it's related to **buoy**.

braccoli   **broccoli**

Braille
This system of printing for people with visual disabilities comes from the name of the inventor, Louis Braille.

brake/break
The first of these homophones involves stopping and the second

Correct spelling	*Incorrect spelling*

involves splitting or cracking. Any confusion in use and spelling usually arises in certain expressions, as "a **break** in the action" (yes, the action stops, but the activity is split) or "those are the **breaks**."

braun	**brawn**
brauny	**brawny**

bravado

brawn, brawny

bread/bred

Bread is what we eat. **Bred** is how we have been conditioned, as a result of breeding or, more usually now, upbringing.

breadth/breath

Breadth is a dimension, from **broad** (hence the *d*). **Breath** is from the verb **breathe**.

break/brake (see entry for **brake/break**)

breakfast

This is the meal with which we **break** our nightly **fast**.

breath/breadth (see entry for **breadth/breath**)

breath, breathe

Some people confuse these related words: just think of **breathe** (the verb) as being spelled with a final –e for easy—and you can **breathe** easy.

breatheren	**brethren**

bred/bread (see entry for **bread/bred**)

breif	**brief**

brethren

brevity

bribe

This word goes back to Middle English, meaning "something stolen," and Middle French, meaning "bread given to a beggar." A question of perspective?

brief

Correct spelling   *Incorrect spelling*

Correct spelling	Incorrect spelling

broccoli

brochette

brocolli   **broccoli**

broshet   **brochette**

building

bulettin   **bulletin**

bulimia

bullabase   **bouillabaisse***

bulletin

bullimia   **bulimia**

bullion/bouillon (see entry for **bouillon/bullion**)

bunion

bunyon   **bunion**

buoyant

bureau/burro

These words are almost homonyms. The first is an office or an agency, borrowed from French. The second is a donkey, borrowed from Spanish.

bureaucracy

burglar, burglarize, burgle

This word comes from an old Germanic word that gives us **burg**, because a **burglar** stole things in town, whereas a highwayman stole things along the thoroughfares. It's easier to spell **burglar** correctly if you think of it as *burg lar*ceny.

burito   **burrito***

burlesque

burrito

This food comes from the Mexican word for "little donkey."

burro/bureau (see entry for **bureau/burro**)

business

byte/bite (see entry for **bite/byte**)

Correct spelling	Incorrect spelling

Incorrect spelling	Correct spelling
cacaphonus	**cacophonous***
cacaphony	**cacophony***

cache/cash
Cache is something that is hidden or a type of computer memory. **Cash** is money. So, if you hide your money, it's a **cash cache**.

cacophonous, cacophony
These words come from a Greek combination of *kakos* (bad) and *phone* (sound).

cadaver

caffeine

calamine

calendar
A friend never misspells this word; he just thinks of the last three letters of this word as standing for *d*ates *a*rranged *r*egularly.

Incorrect spelling	Correct spelling
callamine	**calamine**
calosal, calossal	**colossal**
camaflage	**camouflage***

camaraderie
There's no **camera** in this word—but almost. The word comes from the Latin word *camera*, meaning "room," which comes into English in **chamber** and **camera**. It developed in French into *camarade*, a roommate or any companion; we have the related **comrade**.

Incorrect spelling	Correct spelling
cameleon	**chameleon***

camera

Incorrect spelling	Correct spelling
cameraderie	**camaraderie***

camouflage

This is a French word pronounced English style, as the French took an Italian word and pronounce and spell it French style. Confusing! Here's a mnemonic for those troublesome first syllables: **c**oncealed **a**nd **m**oving **o**penly **u**ndetected.

campaign

camra	**camera**

cancel, cancellation, cancelled

candadate	**candidate***
candal	**candle**
candalabra	**candelabra***
candel	**candle**

candelabra

This is the plural of the rarely used *candelabrum*, "candlestick," which comes from the Latin, *candela*, which also comes into English as **candle**.

cander	**candor**

candidate

You might remember the spelling of this word if you think of a **candidate** as being **candid**. (Sure, that's very rare!) Actually, that's close to the origins of this word. It comes from the Latin, *candidatus*, meaning "clothed in white," since candidates for office in ancient Rome dressed in white togas.

candle

candleabra	**candelabra***

candor

canine

cansel	**cancel**
canselation, cansellation	**cancellation**

cantaloupe

This melon comes from northern India, but it was named after *Cantalupo*, a former papal villa near Rome, and the name passed into English through French.

Correct spelling	*Incorrect spelling*

cantankerous
> This word makes etymologists disagreeable, since they can't be sure of the origin. The most likely explanation is that it derived from a Middle English word, *contack* or *contek*, meaning "contentious."

cantelope	**cantaloupe**
canumdrum	**conumdrum***

canvas/canvass
> **Canvas** is a type of fabric. **Canvass** is a verb meaning "to examine" or, more usually, "to survey" or a noun meaning "examination," "discussion," "solicitation," or "survey."

canvass/canvas (see entry for **canvas/canvass**)

capachino	**cappuccino***

capacious

capacity

capascious	**capacious**
capasity	**capacity**
capatious	**capacious**

capital/capitol
> **Capital** is the city where the center of government is located; think of the final *–al* as standing for *a* location. **Capitol** is the building that houses the legislators; think of the *o* as representing the *o* in dome.

capitol/capital (see entry for **capital/capitol**)

cappuccino
> This word is Italian, for "Capuchin monk," because the color of the coffee resembled the color of the monks' habits.

caprice, capricious

capsule

caracature	**caricature***
carage	**carriage**
carasel	**carousel**

Correct spelling	*Incorrect spelling*

carasine	**kerosene***
carassel	**carousel**

carat/caret/carrot/karat

A **carat** is a unit of weight for precious stones or gold, a variant of **karat** (which is why it's abbreviated as "K"). A **caret** is a proofreading symbol used to indicate where something is to be inserted in a text. (Think of the –e- as standing for **error**.) A **carrot** is similar to its homophones only in that it's something that's not quite gold that you insert in your mouth.

carcass

carcinogen

carcinoma

carcuss	**carcass**

cardiovascular

caret/carat/carrot (see entry for **carat/caret/carrot**)

cariage	**carriage**

Caribbean

The first syllable of this word is easy to spell. Then it's just **rib** and **bean**.

caricature

This word traveled around western Europe. English got it from French, which borrowed it from Italian, where it meant "the act of loading a cart." The root is Latin for "cart," a word that came from Celtic. It's related to the verb **carry** and (through Old French) **charge** and (through Spanish) **cargo**. But what does a **cart** have to do with a **caricature**? That's a question for etymologists to debate.

carisma	**charisma**

carousel

This is the standard spelling. A variant spelling is **carrousel**.

carpal

carrage	**carriage**
carrcass	**carcass**

Correct spelling	*Incorrect spelling*

carriage

Carribbean, Carribean   **Caribbean***

carricature   **caricature***

carrot/carat/caret (see entry for **carat/caret/carrot**)

carroussel   **carousel***

carsinogen   **carcinogen**

carsinoma   **carcinoma**

caset   **cassette**

cash/cache (see entry for **cache/cash**)

cashmere
> You can remember the spelling for this pricey fabric by thinking of the money spent for it as "**mere cash**." The name **cashmere** came from *Kashmir*, a region in India in the Himalayas where the goats are found that provide the wool.

cassette

castigate

castle

cataclysm, cataclysmic

catagorical   **categorical**

catagory   **category**

catalog, catalogue

catalyst, catalytic

catapiller   **caterpillar***

catapult

catastrophe, catastrophic
> This word is Greek, from a word meaning "to overturn"—as when our lives are totally upset.

categorical, categorize, category

catelog, catelogue   **catalog, catalogue**

caterpillar
> This word came into Old English from Old North French, with some twists and turns. The French called it a *catepelose*, "hairy

cat"(!?). That probably made little sense to the English, except that the words resembled the two Old English words *cater* (glutton) and *piller* (thief). So the name remained, but with a change in meaning.

catharsis, cathartic

Incorrect spelling	Correct spelling
cattaclysm	**cataclysm**
cattaclysmic	**cataclysmic**
cattagorical	**categorical**
cattagory	**category**
cattalist	**catalyst**
cattalitic	**catalytic**
cattalog, cattalogue	**catalog, catalogue**
cattalyst, cattalytic	**catalyst, catalytic**
cattapiller	**caterpillar***
cattapult	**catapult**
cattastrophe	**catastrophe**
cattastrophic	**catastrophic***
cattegorical	**categorical**
cattegorize	**categorize**
cattegory	**category**
cattelog, cattelogue	**catalog, catalogue**
catterpillar, catterpiller	**caterpillar***

cauliflower

caustic

This word comes from the Greek *–caust*, from the word for "to burn," a root also found in **holocaust** and (slightly modified) **cauterize**.

cavalier

caveat

This word is straight Latin, "beware," as in the expression *caveat emptor*—"let the buyer beware."

cedar

Correct spelling	*Incorrect spelling*

cede/seed

Cede means "to surrender, grant, or transfer." **Seed** is something that is planted or the act of planting.

ceiling

You can apply the old "*i* before *e* except after *c*" rule here. Or you can correctly spell the problematic first syllable by just thinking of the instructions Michelangelo received for painting the Sistine Chapel **ceiling**—"**C**over every *i*nch."

Incorrect spelling	Correct spelling
celabrate	**celebrate**
celabration	**celebration**
celabratory	**celebratory**
celar	**cellar***
celary	**celery***

celebrate, celebration, celebratory

celery/salary

You're not likely to confuse these homophones. The word **salary** comes from Latin, *salarium*, "salt allowance." In Roman times, part of the wages paid to soldiers included an allowance to buy salt (*sal*), a necessary part of the diet and used to preserve food. The word **celery** for a vegetable that tastes better with an allowance of salt came into English through French and Italian from the Latin word for "parsley."

celibacy, celibate

Incorrect spelling	Correct spelling
cellabrate	**celebrate**
cellabration	**celebration**
cellabratory	**celebratory**

cellar/seller

A **cellar** is a basement, from the Latin *cellarium*, "storeroom." A **seller** is someone who sells something.

Incorrect spelling	Correct spelling
cellebrate	**celebrate**
cellebration	**celebration**
cellebratory	**celebratory**
cellibacy, cellibasy	**celibacy**

Correct spelling	*Incorrect spelling*

cellibate	**celibate**
cellular	
cematary	**cemetery**
cement	
cemetery	
cemment	**cement**

censor/censure

These quasi homophones are sometimes confused. **Censor** is a person who suppresses something deemed objectionable or it's the action of suppressing. (Think of the *–or* as standing for "**o**bjectionable *r*eference.") **Censure** is a noun or a verb denoting blame or disapproval. (Think of the *–u-* as standing for "**u**nacceptable.")

censure/censor (see entry for **censor/censure**)

centenarian

centennial

center

Although some people seem to believe that it's stylish or classy to use the British *–re* spelling of this word for retail or housing complexes, American usage still holds for **center**.

centrifugal, centrifuge

cercumcise	**circumcise**
cercumcision	**circumcision**
cercumference	**circumference***
cercumlocution	**circumlocution**
cercumnavigate	**circumnavigate**
cercumspect	**circumspect**
cercumvent	**circumvent**

cereal/serial

Cereal is a grain or a food made from a grain. **Serial** describes a series or things in a series.

cerebral

ceremonial, ceremonious, ceremony

Correct spelling	*Incorrect spelling*

certafy   **certify**

certificate

certify

challenge

chameleon

    The Greeks gave us the name of this lizard, combining the words for "on the ground" and "lion."

chamois

chanal   **channel**

chandelier

chanel   **channel**

change, changeable, changing

channel

chaperon or **chaperone**

    Chaperon is French for "hood," for the head covering typically worn by **chaperons** in centuries past.

chariot

charisma, charismatic

charriot   **chariot**

chastise

chauffeur

    This word, as you might guess from the pronunciation and the –*eur* ending, is French, from a verb meaning "to stoke the fire," from an era when drivers did more than turn an ignition key.

chauvinism, chauvinist

    Chauvinism, which originally meant "fanatical patriotism," comes from French, named after a legendary French soldier.

chef

cheif   **chief**

chic/sheik

    Chic is fashionable (and it's not pronounced "chick"). A **sheik** is an Arabic leader, from an Arabic word meaning "old man."

Correct spelling   *Incorrect spelling*

chief

chivalrous, chivalry

chlamydia

chlorine

cholesterol

choose/chose

Choose is present tense and **chose** is past tense. These words are not homophones, but they're sometimes confused.

chow/ciao

Chow is the slang term for food or a breed of dog. **Ciao** is the Italian goodbye, which is easy to spell—if you know that the *ci* in Italian sounds like the *ch* in English. Then it's just a quick *a* and *o*.

chrisalis, chriselis	**chrysalis**
chrisanthemum	**chrysanthemum**

chrome

chronic

This word comes through French from the Greek word for "time," a root we find in such words as **chronicle**, **chronology**, and **chronometer**.

chrysalis

chrysanthemum

ciao/chow (see entry for **chow/ciao**)

cicle, ciclical	**cycle, cyclical***
cieling	**ceiling***
ciffilis	**syphilis**
cinamon, cinamun	**cinnamon**

cinch

cinic	**cynic***
cinical	**cynical***

cinnamon

cinnic	**cynic***
cinnical	**cynical***

Correct spelling	*Incorrect spelling*

circuit, circuitous, circuitry

circulatory

circumcise, circumcision

circumference

This word is from Latin, *circum,* "around"—as in **circumstance,** **circumspect**, and **circumlocution**—and the verb meaning "to carry"—as in **refer** (and **reference**), **prefer** (and **preference**), **confer** (and **conference**), and **defer** (and **deference**). That pattern may help you remember the spelling of **circumference**.

circumlocution

circumnavigate

circumspect

circumvent

circut   **circuit**

cirrhosis

cite/sight/site

To **cite** is to mention, to reference. **Sight** is something seen or the ability to see. **Site** is a location, such as a Web site, where something is *sit*uated.

clamidia   **chlamydia**

clandestine

classic

claustrophobia

This is a linguistic combination—the first half comes from Latin, *claustrum* (enclosed place) and the second half comes from Greek, *phobia* (fear).

clearance

cliché

This word is French, originally meaning "a plate" as used in a printing process known as **stereotype**.

click/clique

A **click** is a noise. A **clique** is an exclusive group. Both words represent the same brief, sharp sound, but **clique** has a French origin and **click** is 100% English.

| **Correct spelling** | *Incorrect spelling* |

clique/click (see entry for **click/clique**)

clone

The science of **cloning** may be new, but this word comes from the Greek word for "twig." The earliest "cloning" was in grafting twigs onto trees.

clorine	**chlorine**
coapious	**copious***

coarse/course

The first of these homophones means "rough" or "indelicate" or "of low quality." The second can mean a lot of things: movement, route, duration, action, succession of activities, body of studies or unit in a body of studies, and core of an idiomatic expression of agreement—"of course." The two words, **coarse** and **course**, seem to have derived from the same Middle English word.

cocanut	**coconut***

cockles

cocoa

coconut

The second part of this word is easy to figure out. The first part, however, is interesting: *coco* is Spanish for "goblin," from the face suggested by the holes on the inner **coconut** shell.

codeine

coerce, coercion

This is a rare noun ending in *–cion*. Another is **suspicion**.

coff	**cough**

cogitate

cognition, cognitive

cognizance, cognizant

This word for "awareness" comes through French from the same Latin verb, meaning "to learn," that evolves into **cognition** and **cognitive**.

cohere, coherent, cohesive

These words come from Latin, from two words stuck together,

| **Correct spelling** | *Incorrect spelling* |

"together" and "to stick" or "to cling." From the root verb we also get **adhere**, **inherent**, and **hesitate**.

coincide, coincidence, coincidental

colaberate, colaborate	**collaborate**
colaflower	**cauliflower**
colage	**collage**

colander

colateral	**collateral**
colege	**college**
colegial	**collegial**
colegiate	**collegiate**
colide	**collide**
coliflower	**cauliflower**
colision	**collision**

collaborate

collaflower	**cauliflower**

collage

collateral

colleague

college

collegial, collegiality

collegiate

collide, collision

An easy way to remember this spelling is to think that you need two *l*'s to cause a **collision**: one alone can't **collide** with itself.

colliflower	**cauliflower**

colloquial

This word comes from two Latin words meaning "to talk with." The first word, *cum*, when it was used as a prefix, took on various spellings, such as *co-* (as in **coeducational**), *com-* (as in **commemorate**), *con-* (as in **conspirator**), or *col-* (as in **colloquial,**

collusion, and **collaborate**).The second word came into English
in such words as **eloquent, loquacious,** and **circumlocution**.

collossal	**colossal**

collude, collusion
> We spell this word with two *l*'s because it comes from two Latin
> words, the prefix *col-* (meaning "with") and the verb *ludere* (play),
> which we also have in the words **prelude, interlude,** and **ludi-
> crous.**

colonel/kernel
> A **colonel** is a military rank or honorary title.The English pro-
> nunciation was influenced by the Spanish word for this rank, *coro-
> nel*. A **kernel** is a grain or seed.

coloquial	**colloquial***

colossal

colude	**collude***
colusion	**collusion***
comemorate	**commemorate**
comensurate	**commensurate***
coment	**comment**
comentary	**commentary**
comentater, comentator	**commentator**
comentery	**commentary**
comerce	**commerce**
comercial	**commercial**

comeuppance

comfort, comfortable

coming
> This is an application of the standard rule for adding *–ing* to a
> verb: if the if the verb ends in an *–e*, drop the *–e* and add *–ing*.

comiserate	**commiserate**
comission	**commission**
comitee	**committee**

Correct spelling	*Incorrect spelling*

comitment	**commitment**
comittee	**committee**

commemorate

commensurate

This word comes almost straight from Latin, *commensuratus*, meaning "measured together," for something measured out in proportion to something else. That word comes from the same root as **measure**, a word that evolved through Old French and Middle English.

comment, commentary, commentator

commerce

comming	**coming***

commiserate

commission

commit

commitee	**committee**

commitment

committee

commoddity	**commodity**

commodious

This word now means "spacious" or "roomy," but it used to just mean "suitable," from Latin words meaning "with" and "measure."

commodity

commonality, commonalty

You have a choice here, although **commonalty** is the preferred spelling.

communicate, communication

community

comodious	**commodious***
comodity	**commodity**

comparative, compare, comparison

Correct spelling	*Incorrect spelling*

compatance, compatence	**competence**
compatant, compatent	**competent***
compel, compelled, compulsion	
compendium	
competative	**competitive***
competence	

competent

This word is easy: it comes from the same Latin words that give us **compete**—and it's a lot easier to **compete** successfully if you're **competent.**

competitive

This word is misspelled because the pronunciation of the third syllable is lax. It's easy to spell correctly if you think of **competition.**

complacent

complament	**complement/**
	compliment*
complamentary	**complementary/**
	complimentary*
complasant, complasent	**complacent**
complection	**complexion**

complement/compliment,
    complementary/complimentary

If you mean something that completes or balances something else, it's **complement, complementary**. If you mean something that pleases and/or is free, it's **compliment, complimentary**.

complexion

Although this word may rhyme with **connection, detection, infection, inspection, protection, rejection,** and so forth, it comes from the Latin *complexio,* which comes from the adjective that gives us **complex**. Remember that root and you should have no problem spelling this word correctly.

Correct spelling   *Incorrect spelling*

compliance, compliant
compromise

comunal	**communal**
comune	**commune**
communicate	**communicate**
comunism	**communism**
comunist	**communist**
comunity	**community**
conaiseur, conaisseur, conaseur,	
conasseur	**connoisseur***

concede, concession
> Only three verbs in English end in –ceed—**exceed, proceed,** and **succeed**—and only one verb ends in –sede—**supersede.** The rest that have this final sound are spelled –cede: **cede, intercede, precede, recede, secede, antecede.**

conceivable
conceive
> The old principle of "*i* before *e* except after *c*" works here.

concensual	**consensual**
concensus	**consensus**

> The core of this word is –sens-, because the word means "feeling together with," as in **consent.**

conception

concience	**conscience***
concientious	**conscientious***
concieve	**conceive***
concious	**conscious**

concise, concision
> This word is from Latin, *concisus*, meaning "cut up." We find the root verb in **precise** and, with a shift in meaning to "kill," in **homicide, suicide,** and **herbicide.**

concoction

| **Correct spelling** | *Incorrect spelling* |

concomitant
> We get this elegant word from Latin for "accompanying," with the root, *comes* (companion), also coming into English in the noble **count** and in **constable**.

condament   **condiment**

condemn, condemnation

condiment

conducive

confascate   **confiscate**

confer, conferred

confidance   **confidence**

confidant, confidante
> This is not someone who is **confident** but someone in whom you **confide**.

confidence, confident

confiscate, confiscation

congenial

conglomerate
> This word comes almost directly from Latin: *conglomeratus* is the past participle of a verb meaning "wound up together in a ball," based on *glomus*, "ball."

congratulate, congratulations

congruence, congruent

connaiseur, connaisseur,
connaseur, connasseur   **connoisseur***

connivance, connive
> The origin of these words is a Latin verb meaning "to close the eyes."

connoisseur
> This French word is spelled in English as the French spelled it more than a century ago. It means someone who knows. We have a related word in **reconnoiter**.

Correct spelling   *Incorrect spelling*

connote, connotation

conoiseur, conoisseur	**connoisseur***
conote	**connote**
conotation	**connotation**
consamate	**consummate**
consaquence	**consequence**
consaquential	**consequential**

conscience, conscientious

These words come from Latin, meaning "with knowledge." The Latin word for knowledge became our word **science**.

conscious

consede	**concede***

consensual

consensus

consential, consentual	**consensual**

consequence, consequential

conshus	**conscious**
consience	**conscience***
consientious	**conscientious***

consign, consignee, consignment

consimate	**consummate**
consious	**conscious**
consiquence	**consequence**
consiquential	**consequential**
consise	**concise***
consision	**concision***

consistence, consistent

consomate	**consummate**
consome	**consommé***
consommate	**consummate**

Correct spelling	*Incorrect spelling*

consommé
> This soup and its name come from French, the past participle of the verb *consommer*, "to use up," from the same Latin root that evolves into **consummate**.

consummate, consummation

contagion, contagious
> These words come from a Latin noun, *contagio*, based on a verb that evolved into our **contact** (and also **contingent** and **contiguous**): diseases and behaviors are **contagious** through **contact**.

contemporary

contemptible

contemptuous

contiguous
> This word means "touching." The **contiguous** U.S. would be the first 48 states, exclusive of Alaska and Hawaii, because their borders don't touch the borders of the other 48. Some people seem to believe that **continental** means the same thing, but that would properly include Alaska—although still exclude Hawaii.

contingency, contingent

continual, continuation, continue, continuity, continuous

contortion
> To spell this word, think of the root word **contort** (and not the related **torsion**).

control, controlling

controversial, controversy

conundrum
> This word is what it means, a riddle or an intricate and difficult problem, since the origin is unknown.

convalescence, convalescent

convenient, convenience

conversant

convertible

| Correct spelling | *Incorrect spelling* |

coordinate

cooth **couth**

copious
This word goes back through Middle English and Old French to the Latin *copia*, "abundance," which is also found in **cornucopia**, a Latin word meaning "horn of plenty," which English borrowed directly.

coragated **corrugated**

cordaroy **corduroy**

cordinate, cordonate **coordinate**

corduroy

corect **correct**

coregated **corrugated**

corespond **correspond**

corespondance, corespondence **correspondence***

corigated **corrugated**

cornucopia

coroberate **corroborate**

corode **corrode***

corogated **corrugated**

corosion **corrosion***

corosive **corrosive***

corragated **corrugated**

correspond

correspondence, correspondent
It's easier to spell the final syllable of these two words correctly if you think of sending **correspondence** to a **correspondent** in an **en**velope.

corrigated **corrugated**

corroborate

corrode, corrosion, corrosive
These words come from the Latin verb, *corrodere*, "to gnaw to pieces," from the verb *rodere*, which evolves into our **rodent** and **erode**.

| **Correct spelling** | *Incorrect spelling* |

corrugated

cough

council/counsel

Council is a noun meaning "meeting" or "advisory or legislative body." A **councilor** is a member of such a body. **Counsel** is a verb meaning "to advise" or a noun meaning "advice." A **counselor** is one who advises.

council, councilor (see entry for **council/counsel**)

counsel/council (see entry for **council/counsel**)

counsel, counselor (see entry for **council/counsel**)

counterfeit

A friend suggests this way to remember the –ei- of the final syllable: to **counterfeit** is to ƒ(ak)**e it**.

coup d'état

course/coarse (see entry for **coarse/course**)

courser/cursor

These words come from the same source, the Latin verb "to run." The first is almost obsolete, meaning "swift horse." The second is a very recent coinage, designating the blinking indicator on a computer screen.

coursery   **cursory***

courtesy

couth

credibility, credible

The root word is Latin, *credo,* meaning "I believe," which comes straight into English as **credo** and indirectly as the synonym **creed,** as well as in **credence, credit,** and **credulous.**

crescendo

This musical term is pure Italian, from a Latin verb that also gives us **crescent, increase, decrease,** and **concrete.**

crevasse

This is the French word for "crevice," of more limited meaning than **crevice.**

| Correct spelling | *Incorrect spelling* |

crevice
>   This word came into Middle English from the Middle French word that would evolve into **crevasse**. The root is a Latin verb meaning "to split."

crevvasse   **crevasse***

crevvice   **crevice***

cringe

crisanthemum   **chrysanthemum**

crisis, crises
>   These words are pure Latin, but borrowed almost unchanged from a Greek noun meaning "decision." The plural is formed as with other Greek nouns ending in *–is*, such as **analysis (analyses)**, **synthesis (syntheses)**, and **metamorphosis (metamorphoses)**

criteria, criterion
>   This word is Greek, slightly modified, which is why the singular ends in *–on* and the plural ends in *–a*.

critical, criticism, criticize, critique

crocadile   **crocodile***

crochaty   **crotchety**

crochet

crocodile
>   This word came from Greek and evolved through Latin, Old French, and Middle English. The Greek root combined "pebble" and "worm" to name this reptile.

croshay   **crochet**

crotchety

crucial
>   This adjective, which we generally use to mean "of critical importance," also means "cross-shaped," showing its origin in the Latin noun, *crux*, which we borrow directly when we talk about "the **crux** of an argument" and which also came into English in such words as **crucify, cruise,** and **excruciating**.

| **Correct spelling** | *Incorrect spelling* |

crucifixion

crushal, crusial   **crucial***

cubicle

cue/queue

> **Cue** is a noun meaning "a prompt or other signal" or a verb meaning "to give a cue." It's also a stick in billiards or pool. **Queue** is "a line" or "a sequence" or "a long braid of hair." It's pure French, which accounts for the odd *–ueue* spelling for a single vowel sound.

cuisine

> This word is French for "cooking" or "kitchen." We often use it with **haute** (high or refined) or **nouvelle** (new).

culprit

cummulative   **cumulative**

cumpendium   **compendium**

cumulative

curcery   **cursory***

curency, curent   **currency, current**

curfew

> This word came into English from a French expression meaning "cover the fire."

curiculum   **curriculum**

curiosity

curmudgeon

currant/current

> A **currant** is a berry much like a raisin. (In fact, the word derives from a Middle English term for "raisins from Corinth," a city in Greece.) **Current** is a noun meaning "a flow of water or electricity" or an adjective meaning "modern" or "recent."

currency, current

curriculum, curriculum vitae

cursor

Correct spelling	*Incorrect spelling*

cursory

This word comes from the Latin, *cursor*, "runner," a word that was recently borrowed for the computer **cursor**. It also comes into English in the words **precursor** and the slightly altered **courser**, while the root verb, *currere*, gives us such words as **current, cursive,** and **curriculum.**

curt

curtesy   **courtesy**

curtail

This word comes from the same Latin root, *curtus*, as **curt**. The spelling of **curtail** reveals its original meaning—"to dock a horse's tail."

cycle, cyclical

These words come, on a cycle through Latin, from the Greek word, *kuklos*, meaning "circle," which we find in **Cyclops** (circle eye) and which may also have been the origin of **cyclone**.

cynic, cynical

This word comes almost directly from Latin, *cynicus*, which seems to have come from the Greek word for "dog." The word was a label for members of a school of philosophy founded by a disciple of Socrates.

Correct spelling   *Incorrect spelling*

daiquiri
: This cocktail was named after *Daiquirí,* a village in Cuba.

dane **deign***
: Unless you're referring to a breed of dog or someone from Denmark, you mean **deign**.

daqueri **daiquiri***

dastardly

daze, dazed, dazzle, dazzled
: **Dazzle** comes from **daze**, which derives from a Middle English verb that came from Old Norse verb meaning "to become exhausted."

debacle

debauched, debauchery

debilitate, debility

debit

debt

decade

decadence, decadent
: These words come from Old French from a medieval Latin word meaning "a falling," from *decadere,* "to fall down." From the same root, by a slightly different route, evolved the word **decay**.

decaffeinated

deceased

decedent
: This is a legal term for someone who's dead. Don't confuse with **decadent**, "in a state of decay or decline."

| **Correct spelling** | *Incorrect spelling* |

deceive, deception
Don't let this word **deceive** you: the old principle of "*i* before *e* except after *c*" works here, as in all verbs that end in *–ceive*.

decelerate

decend   **descend**

decesed   **deceased**

deciduous

decieve   **deceive***

decrescendo
This musical term is pure Italian, from a Latin verb that also gives us **crescent**, **increase**, **decrease**, and **concrete**.

deduct, deductible, deduction

defendant, defense
Only a few words end in *–ense:* **defense**, **dense**, **expense**, **immense**, **offense**, and **pretense**.

defer, deference, deferential, deferred

define, definite, definitely, definition

dehydrate, dehydration

deign
This word meaning "to condescend reluctantly" comes from an Old French verb, *deignier*, that also (with a slight change in spelling) gave us **disdain**. The origin of these words was the Latin adjective, *dignus* (worthy), that evolves into our **dignified** and **dignity** as well as **indignant**.

déjà vu
This expression is straight French, meaning "already seen."

delectable

delicacy, delicate

delicatessen

delicious

delineate

deliscious   **delicious**

dellicacy   **delicacy**

| Correct spelling | *Incorrect spelling* |

dellicate	**delicate**
delliccatessen	**delicatessen**
dellicious	**delicious**

deluxe

demagogue, demagoguery
These words come from Greek, *demagogos*, from *demos* (common people)—as in **democracy, demographics**, and **endemic**—and *agogos* (leading), as in **pedagogue**.

demise

demoralize

dence	**dense**
dencity	**density**

denigrate, denigration
These words come from a Latin verb based on the adjective, *niger*, meaning "black."

denomination

denotation, denote

dense, density

dependence, dependent

depreciate, depreciation
Depreciate and its antonym, **appreciate**, go back to the Latin noun, *pretium*, meaning "price." In addition to **price**, this root evolved into **prize, precious**, and **praise**.

derable, derible	**durable***

derelict

deress	**duress***

deride
This word and the related **derision, derisive,** and **derisory** come from the Latin verb, *ridere*, "to laugh," which is also the root of **ridiculous**.

de rigueur
The expression **de rigueur** is pure French, "required by fashion or custom, socially obligatory."

Correct spelling	*Incorrect spelling*

derilict	**derelict**

derision, derisive, derisory

derogative, derogatory

derrable, derrible	**durable***
derralict	**derelict**
derress	**duress***
derrogative	**derogative**
derrogatory	**derogatory**

descend, descendant, descent

describe, description

desecrate, desecration

> The core of these words is the Latin, *sacr-*, "sacred," as in **consecrate.**

desend	**descend**

desert/dessert

> A friend remembers **dessert** in this way: she thinks of the psychological effect of the calories in **desserts,** which is **stressed** spelled backwards. As for **desert**, think of the single *s* as standing for the *s*and.

desiduous	**deciduous**

design, designate, designation

desirable, desire, desirous

> These words come from the Old French verb, *desirer*, from the Latin *desiderare*, from the root *sidus*, meaning "star." That root comes into English as well in the erudite adjective **sidereal** and in **consider.**

despair

desperate, desperation

> These words are related to **despair**, of course, but that verb came from Latin through Old French and Middle English, which changed the spelling, while **desperate** came from Latin directly.

despicable, despise

> **Despise** is one of 11 commonly misspelled verbs ending in *–ise.* The others are **advertise, advise, apprise, chastise, devise,**

Correct spelling	*Incorrect spelling*

exercise, improvise, revise, supervise, and surprise.

despondent

dessert/desert (see entry for **desert/dessert**)

destination, destine, destiny

destroy, destruction, destructive

det   **debt**

détente
>   This word is pure French, from the same Latin verb that gave us **distend**.

deter, deterrent, deterring
>   **Deter** comes from a Latin verb that means "to frighten away," from the same root as **terror, terrify, terrible**, and **terrific**.

detriment, detrimental

devastate, devastation

develop, development, developmental

deveous   **devious**

device/devise
>   **Device** is "a scheme" or "a mechanism." **Devise** is "to invent" or "to plot."

devious

devise/device (see entry for **device/devise**)

devistate   **devastate**

devistation   **devastation**

devour
>   This word comes from the Latin *devorare*, "to devour." The base of that verb developed into **voracious**.

dexterity, dexterous
>   These words perpetuate an ageless bias against lefthanders: they come from the Latin, *dexter*, meaning "right-handed."

diafram   **diaphragm**

diagnosis, diagnostic
>   This word comes from two Greek words meaning "to know apart." The second root word is also found in **prognosis**

Correct spelling	*Incorrect spelling*

("knowing in advance") and **prognosticate** ("to know in advance, to predict").

dialysis

diameter, diametrical, diametrically

These words come from a Greek word meaning "to measure through," which is what we do across a circle, with the opposite ends of the **diameter** giving rise to our meaning of **diametrical** and **diametrically**.

diaphragm

diarea   **diarrhea***

diarrhea

This word comes from a Greek verb, *diarrhein*, meaning "to flow through." The root of that verb, *rheos* (stream) comes into English in technical and scientific words such as **rheostat** and **rheology**.

diary

diatribe

dichotomous, dichotomy

These words come directly from Greek, from an adjective that means "divided in two."

diciple   **disciple***

diciplinarian   **disciplinarian***

diciplinary   **disciplinary***

dicipline   **discipline***

diction, dictionary

didactic, didacticism

die, dying

Verbs that end in *–ie* generally change to *–y* when taking the suffix *–ing*.

difacult, difecult   **difficult***

differ, difference, differential, differentiate

difficult, difficulty

These words come from the Latin adjective, *difficilis*, "not easy," from the same root that evolved into **facile** and **facility**.

Correct spelling	*Incorrect spelling*

digit, digital

dilagance, dilageance, dilagence   **diligence**

dilettante

This word gives some people trouble because it comes straight from Italian (delighting). Here's a mnemonic to help with the tricky beginning syllables: "*d*abbles *i*n *l*iterally *e*very *t*empting *t*hing."

diligence, diligent

dillatant, dillatante, dilletant, dilletante   **dilettante***

dilligance, dilligeance, dilligence   **diligence**

diminish

diminutive

dimminish   **diminish**

dimminutive   **diminutive**

dinasaur   **dinosaur**

dining

Some people have trouble with this word, perhaps because of the double *n* in **dinner**. But the formation of this word follows the rule: if the verb ends in an —e, drop the —e and add —*ing*.

dinosaur

diphtheria

disability, disable, disabled

disagree

disapear   **disappear**

disapoint   **disappoint***

disappear, disappearance

disappoint

This word is easier to spell if you remember that it comes from a Latin verb that meant the opposite (*dis*) of "appoint," with the original meaning of "remove from office."

disarray

disaster, disastrous

These words come to us from Latin, *dis-* (a pejorative prefix) and *astrum* (star). We have the meaning when we talk of "star-crossed" lovers.

| **Correct spelling** | *Incorrect spelling* |

disatisfied	**dissatisfied**
disatisfy	**dissatisfy**

discern, discernment

disciple, disciplinarian, disciplinary, discipline
These words all come from the Latin verb, *discere*, "to learn."

disconcert

discreet/discrete, discretion
Discreet means prudent, tactful, or modest, showing **discretion**.
You can think of the –ee– as representing the core of **feeling**.
Discrete means distinct or separate. Just think of the *t* keeping
the first e separate from the second e.

discrete/discreet (see entry for **discreet/discrete**)

discretion, discretionary

discriminate

disect	**dissect**
disemanate, diseminate, disemmanate,	
disemminate	**disseminate**
disengenuous	**disingenuous**
disension	**dissension***
disent	**dissent***
disertation	**dissertation**
disfunctional	**dysfunctional***

disgruntled

disheveled
This word entered Middle English from an Old French verb meaning "to disarrange the hair," with the roots of that hair being the
Latin *capillus* (hair), which came into English more directly in **cap-
illary**.

disidence	**dissidence**
disident	**dissident***

disingenuous

disinherit

Correct spelling	*Incorrect spelling*

disintegrate
disinterested

Incorrect spelling	**Correct spelling**
disipate	**dissipate**
disipation	**dissipation***
disiple	**disciple***
disiplinarian	**disciplinarian***
disiplinary	**disciplinary***
disipline	**discipline***
dislexia	**dyslexia***
dislexic	**dyslexic***

dismiss, dismissal

disonance	**dissonance***
disonant	**dissonant***

disparage

    This verb comes from Middle English, where *disparagen* meant "to degrade," which evolved through Old French from a Latin root, *parage*, "rank," from a noun meaning "peer." So, to **disparage**, then and now, is to treat somebody as being inferior.

dispel

    This word is easier to spell if you keep in mind that it breaks into two parts, both from Latin, *dis-* (apart) and *–pel* (to drive, as in **compel** and **repel**).

dispensable, dispense

    The root of these words is the Latin verb *dispendere*, "to weigh out." We have related words in **compensate** and **recompense**.

dissability	**disability**
dissable	**disable**
dissabled	**disability**
dissagree	**disagree**
dissapear, dissappear	**disappear**
dissaperance, dissappearance	**disappearance**
dissapline	**discipline**

Correct spelling	*Incorrect spelling*

Correct / Incorrect	
dissapoint, dissappoint	**disappoint***
dissarray	**disarray**
dissatisfied, dissatisfy	
dissconcert	**disconcert**
dissect	
dissedence	**dissidence***
dissedent	**dissident***
disseminate	
dissension, dissent	

In these words we find the Latin prefix *dis-* (apart) and verb *sentire* (to feel).

dissern	**discern**
dissertation	
dissfunctional	**dysfunctional***
dissidence, dissident	

These words come from the Latin verb, *dissidere*, "to disagree," with the original meaning being "to sit apart."

dissingenuous	**disingenuous**
dissintegrate	**disintegrate**
dissinterested	**disinterested**
dissipate, dissipation	

The Latin origin of this word was *dissipare*, "to disperse" or "to scatter," from *dis-* (apart) and *supare* (to throw).

dissipline	**discipline***
disslexia	**dyslexia***
disslexic	**dyslexic***
dissmisal, dissmissal	**dismissal**
dissmiss	**dismiss**
dissonance, dissonant	

The Latin prefix *dis-* means "apart" and the root verb *sonare* means "to sound," a root that we find with the prefix *con-* (together) in the antonym, **consonant.**

disstil, disstill	**distill**

Correct spelling   *Incorrect spelling*

disstilation   **distillation**

dissuade

> The Latin prefix *dis-* here means "away" and the root verb, *suadere*, means "to advise," a verb we also find in **persuade** and **suasion**.

distill, distillation, distilled

distraught

> **Distraught** is a Middle English variant of the past participle of *distracten*, with its meaning now much stronger than **distracted**. The Latin root of the verb meant "to draw apart," from a verb that we find evolving into such words as **detract**, **retraction**, **subtract**, and **tractor**.

disuade, diswade   **dissuade***

diverse

diversion, divert

dobious   **dubious**

doc/dock

> The first of these homophones is a short form of **doctor**. The second is a pier, the space between two piers, to put a ship alongside a dock, or to clip short or cut off (e.g., a tail) or to reduce pay.

docile, docility

> These words came straight from Latin, *docilis*, from the verb *docere*, meaning "to teach," which also comes into English in **doctrine**, **indoctrinate**, and **doctor**.

dock/doc (see entry for **doc/dock**)

doldrums

> This word for "mild depression" is also used for ocean regions near the equator characterized by calm weather or only light winds—a source of **doldrums** for sailors far from port. The word comes from Old English, *dol*, meaning "dull" and also found in **dolt**.

domain

dormant

Correct spelling   *Incorrect spelling*

dormitory

dosile, dosle, dossile, dossle   **docile***

dour/dower

> **Dour** means stern, gloomy, ill-humored. **Dower** is a dowry or the act of providing a dowry.

dower/dour (see entry for **dour/dower**)

draconian

> This adjective we owe to Draco, a legislator in ancient Greece (7th century B.C., to be exact) whose laws were considered very harsh.

Dramamine

droll

drunkenness

> This word is easy if you remember that it's a normal formation from the adjective **drunken** and the noun suffix *–ness*.

dual/duel/duo

> These three homophones (or nearly) all mean "two." **Dual** is generally an adjective (double, composed of two parts). **Duel** is a combat or conflict between two parties. **Duo** is musical, two people singing or playing music together.

dubious

duel/dual/duo (see entry for **dual/duel/duo**)

duffel

> This word comes from the Dutch, for a fabric named after Duffel, a town in Belgium.

du jour

> This expression is French for "of the day." The second word we find in a few words in English, such as **journal** and **adjourn.**

dunce

dungeon

duo/dual/duel (see entry for **dual/duel/duo**)

durability, durable

> The Latin verb *durare* (to last) gave us this word as well as **duration** and **endure.**

| **Correct spelling** | *Incorrect spelling* |

duress

This word (constraint, coercion, harshness) comes from an Old French word meaning "hardness," from a Latin adjective, *durus* (hard), related to the verb that evolved into **durable** and **endure**. It's now generally used only in the expression "under **duress**."

| *durrable, durrible* | **durable*** |
| *durress* | **duress*** |

dysfunctional

The prefix *dys-* is Greek for "abnormal" or "bad."

dyslexia, dyslexic

This word is from two Greek words: *dys-* (abnormal, impaired, difficult, or bad) and *—lexia* (from *lexis*, words).

earring
This is one word (**earring**), not two (*ear ring*).

ecanacea   **echinacea**

eccentric, eccentricity
The origin of these words is anything but eccentric. The medieval Latin word *eccentricus* comes from a Greek word meaning "out of center."

eccinasia   **echinacea**

ecentric   **eccentric***

ecentricity   **eccentricity***

echinacea

eclectic, eclecticism
This word, which we generally use to mean "consisting of things from diverse sources," can also mean "choosing the best," which was the original meaning, from a Greek adjective meaning "selective," from root words meaning "out" and "to choose."

eclipse
The Latin root, *eclipticus*, comes from a Greek word meaning "to fail to appear."

ecstasy, ecstatic
No matter what those X-rated movie teasers may suggest, there's no *x* in **ecstasy**.

ect.   **etc.***

edible

eek   **eke***

Unless you mean the exclamation of surprise caused by a mouse or other creepy, crawly thing, the spelling you want is **eke**, meaning "to supplement" or "to earn with great effort."

Correct spelling	*Incorrect spelling*

Correct spelling	Incorrect spelling
	efective → **effective**
	efemeral → **ephemeral***

effect/affect

   Effect can also be a verb, meaning "to cause or bring about," but it's generally a noun, meaning "result." **Affect** is a verb meaning "to act on, to influence."

effective, effectiveness

effemeral → **ephemeral***

efficacious, efficacy

   These words came directly from Latin, from words based on the verb *efficere*, "to cause," which we also have in the adjectives **efficient** (with a shift in meaning) and **effective** and in the verbs **effectuate** and **effect**.

efficiency, efficient

effusion, effusive

eficacious → **efficacious***

eficacy → **efficacy***

eficient → **efficient**

e.g.

   This expression is hard to misspell, but easy to misuse. It's an abbreviation of *exempli gratia*, Latin meaning "for the sake of an example."

egalitarian, egalitarianism

egregious

   This word means "exceptionally bad," but the original meaning wasn't necessarily negative: the Latin *egregius* meant "distinguished," from the prefix *ex-* (out of) and the root *grex*, meaning "a flock or herd." The root is also found in **gregarious** (which originally meant "belonging to a herd or flock"), **congregation, segregate,** and **aggregate.** The name **Gregory** meant "vigilant" or "watchful" in late Greek, probably a good virtue for guarding a herd or a flock.

Correct spelling	*Incorrect spelling*

eight/ate (see entry for **ate/eight**)

eight, eighteen, eighth, eightieth, eighty

These words cause some spelling problems, but they're all quite logical—except that the suffixes –*teen* and –*th* don't cause a double *t* and the *y* in **eighty** changes to an *i* with the suffix –*eth*.

either

This is one of six exceptions to the *i* before *e* except after *c* rule. The others are **neither**, **leisure**, **seize** and **seizure**, and **weird**.

eke

This word, meaning "to supplement" or "to earn with great effort," comes from a Middle English verb, *eken*, "to increase." Curiously, this word also evolved into **nickname:** the Middle English *ekename* (additional name or increased name) in usage caused confusion, so "an *ekename*" became "a *nekename*" and the rest is history.

eklips	**eclipse**
ekstasy	**ecstasy**
ekwip	**equip**
elafant	**elephant**

This animal was *elephantus* in Latin, from a Greek root.

elagance	**elegance***
elagant	**elegant***
elagy	**elegy**
elamentary	**elementary**
elaphant	**elephant**
elaquant, elaquent	**eloquent***
elbatross, elbetross	**albatross***

electrolysis

elegance, elegant

These words come from Latin: the root verb, *elegare*, meant "to pick out," so **elegant** meant "choosy" and then the meaning evolved into "tasteful" or "refined."

Correct spelling	*Incorrect spelling*

Incorrect spelling	Correct spelling
elegibility	**eligibility***
elegible	**eligible***

elegy

elementary

elephant

| *elequant, elequent* | **eloquent*** |

elicit/illicit

    Elicit with an e means to bring out, as in **evoke**. **Illicit** with an *i* means **illegal**.

eligible, eligibility

    These words come from a Latin adjective, *eligibilis*, from the Latin verb that evolves into **elect**.

eliminate

elipses	**ellipses***
elipsis	**ellipsis***
eliptical	**elliptical***
ellafant	**elephant**
ellagance	**elegance***
ellagant	**elegant***
ellegy	**elegy**
ellephant	**elephant**
ellequant, ellequent	**eloquent***
elligibility	**eligibility***
elligible	**eligible***

ellipses, ellipsis, elliptical

    These words are from the Greek, as we might guess from the singular ending *–is* becoming *–es* in the plural, like **analysis (analyses)**, **crisis (crises)**, and **synthesis (syntheses)**. The root adjective meant "defective," from a verb meaning "to fall short." So, when we shorten a quote, making it "defective," we insert **ellipses** ... and think fondly of the Greeks.

| *ellongated* | **elongated** |

Correct spelling	*Incorrect spelling*

elloquant, elloquent   **eloquent***

ellude, ellusive   **elude, elusive***

elongated

eloquent
> This word is now used for quality of speech, but it comes from the Latin verb that meant "to speak out." Maybe in this respect, at least, practice makes perfect?

elude/allude (see entry for **allude/elude**)

elude, elusive
> These words were more fun in Latin: the verb *eludere* was composed of the prefix *ex-* (away from) and *ludere*, "to play," a root we find in **prelude, ludicrous,** and **allude**—which now means "to make an indirect reference," but which was more originally more lighthearted.

emaciated

embarrass

embassy
> This word comes into English from French, where *em-* and *am-* are usually pronounced the same—which explains why the **em**bassy is home to an ***am**bassador*.

embezzle

embrace

embroglio   **imbroglio**

embryo, embryonic

emend/amend
> **Emend** is usually used only for improving a text. **Amend** is a more general word meaning "to improve."

emerge
> This word came from Latin, from the prefix *ex-* (out of) and the verb *mergere* (to immerse). Our **merge** came from this word, of course, while **immerse** came from the past participle of a related word, *immergere*.

emergency

Correct spelling   *Incorrect spelling*

emergent

emeritus

This Latin word used to indicate an honorary title held by somebody who has retired comes from a verb meaning "to earn,"
which is the root of **merit**.

eminent/imminent, eminence/imminence

Eminent means outstanding or distinguished. **Imminent** means
about to occur.

emmend	**emend***
emmergency	**emergency**
emminent	**eminent***

emollient

An **emollient** makes something softer or smoother, from a Latin
verb, *emollire*, based on the adjective *mollis* (soft), which also came
into English in the verb **mollify**.

empathetic, empathy

empirical, empiricism, empiricist

These words derived from the Latin adjective, *empiricus*, which
came from a Greek adjective meaning "experienced," from a verb
that's the root of **experience**.

empower

enable

enact

enamored

A person who's **enamored** of someone or something may not
be thinking of the origins of this word, but it came into Middle
English from Old French, deriving from the Latin *amor*.

encapsulate

enchilada

This word comes from Mexico, meaning "seasoned with chili pepper."

enciclapedia	**encyclopedia**

encourage, encouragement, encouraging

The heart of the verb **encourage** goes back, by way of Middle
English and Old French, to the Latin *cor*, meaning "heart."

Correct spelling	*Incorrect spelling*

encyclopedia

endeavor

endemic
>   This word for "prevalent in a particular locality or people" comes from the Greek *endemos*, based on the word *demos*, meaning "people."

endever, endevor **endeavor**

energetic, energy

enervate
>   This word, which is often misused, takes its meaning of "to deprive of strength or vitality" from the Latin root words, *ex-* (out) and *nervus* (sinew). The related word, **nerves**, has lost the strength and vitality of that earlier meaning, now being used generally in terms of the nervous system or feelings.

engender

engine

engineer, engineering

enginuity **ingenuity**
>   Although an **engineer** may be known for **ingenuity**, these words have different roots. **Ingenuity** goes back to the same root as **ingenuous**.

enigma, enigmatic
>   There's nothing enigmatic about the origins of these words. They came through Latin from a Greek verb meaning "to speak in riddles."

en masse

ennable	**enable**
ennact	**enact**
ennamored	**enamored***
ennergetic	**energetic**
ennervate	**enervate***
ennumerate	**enumerate***

Correct spelling *Incorrect spelling*

Incorrect spelling	Correct spelling
ennumeration	**enumeration***
ennunciate	**enunciate**
ennunciation	**enunciation**
enquire	**inquire**
enquiry	**inquiry**
enroll	
ensure	
entamologist	**entomologist***
entamology	**entomology***
enterance	**entrance**
enterprener, enterpreneur, enterprenuer	**entrepreneur***

enthrall, enthralled

We use this word to mean "captivated," but the roots show a darker side. The Middle English root meant "in bondage," from the noun *thral*, "slave." But our synonym **captivated** came from the same Latin roots as **captive** and **captured**, so there's a darker side there, too.

entomologist, entomology

The spelling of this word won't bug you if you remember that it comes from the Greek *entomon*, "insect," which was named for its segmented body, from a verb that meant "to cut." We don't use this Greek root in other words, since we've borrowed from the Latin, *insectum*—which also means "cut."

entourage

entrepreneur

This is a French word, from *entreprendre* (to undertake). The *–eur* ending denotes somebody who does something.

Incorrect spelling	Correct spelling
enturage	**entourage**

enumerate, enumeration

These words are easy to spell if you know that they come from a Latin verb, *enumerare*, composed of the prefix e- (from ex-, "out") and the verb *numerus* (number).

enunciate, enunciation

Correct spelling	*Incorrect spelling*

entranse	**entrance**

enviable

environment

An easy way to remember how to spell this word is to think of the word **iron** hidden in it, as **iron** is hidden in our environment. This word has become very important in recent years, but it dates back through the centuries, to an Old French word *environ*, meaning "around"—which we find in the word **environs**—from a verb that meant "to turn around," which may have been Celtic in origin. So this word for what surrounds us came into English in a roundabout way.

envy

epademic, epademmic	**epidemic**
epasode	**episode***
epasodic	**episodic***
epedemic	
epesode	**episode***

ephemeral

This adjective comes from the Greek *ephemeros*, meaning "daily" or "lasting for a day."

epidemic

epiphany

This may be no sudden revelation, but this word developed out of the Greek word *epiphaneia*, which meant "appearance" or "manifestation." The root verb, *phainein*, "to show," appears in **phenomenon**, becomes manifest in **fantasy**, is somewhat veiled in **diaphanous**, is on show in **phantom**, and seems transparent in the recent creation, **cellophane**.

episode, episodic

The first syllables of these two words are a Greek prefix, here meaning "in addition." We find this prefix (with various meanings) in such words as **epidemic, epigram,** and **epitome**.

epitamy	**epitome***

epitaph

Correct spelling	*Incorrect spelling*

epitemy   **epitome***

epithet

epitome
   We use this word to mean "a perfect example," but another
   meaning is "a brief summary," which is the original meaning, coming from a Greek verb meaning "to cut short." The root verb, *tem-*
   nein, "to cut," crawls its way into English in **entomology**, through
   the Greek word for "insect," which meant "cut up," as in the seg-
   ments that characterize insect bodies.

equalibrium   **equilibrium**

equanimity
   We got this word for "composure" directly from Latin, from a
   noun that combined *aequus* (even, equal) and *animus* (mind or
   spirit). The first of these words we recognize in **equilibrium**
   (originally "level balance") and the second lives on (barely) in
   pusillanimous, a fancy way of saying "cowardly" (originally "weak
   spirit").

equanox   **equinox**

equate, equation

equenox   **equinox**

equilibrium

equinimity   **equanimity***

equinox

equip, equipment, equipped

equitable, equity

equivocal
   In this word we should recognize **vocal** and the prefix *equi-*,
   meaning "equal." Words that could have more than one interpre-
   tation and are possibly meant to mislead speak "in equal voices."
   Well, at least that's how the Romans thought.

eradicate
   This word is rooted in the Latin verb *eradicare*, which combined
   the prefix *ex-* (out) and the noun *radix* (root), a word that grew
   into **radical** and **radish**.

Correct spelling   *Incorrect spelling*

Incorrect spelling	Correct spelling

erand · **errand**

Just think of the double *r* in this word as standing for "*r*unning 'round" doing **errands**. (The word comes from an Old English word that meant "business"—interesting, but that won't help you spell it.)

erase, eraser, erasure

These words confuse people because we think of getting rid of **errors**. But these words have their roots in a Latin verb that also gives us **eradicate**.

erect

ering · **earring***

erode, erosion, erosive

These words come from the Latin verb, *erodere*, "to eat away," from the verb *rodere*, "to gnaw," which evolved into our **rodent** and **corrode**.

eroneous, eronious · **erroneous**

erradicate · **eradicate***

errand

errase · **erase***

erraser · **eraser***

errasure · **erasure***

erratic, erratically

This word is easier to spell if you remember that it's based on the verb **err**, to be wrong or to wander.

errect · **erect**

errode · **erode***

erroneous

errosion · **erosion***

errosive · **erosive***

ersatz

erstwhile

erudite, erudition

You don't need to be learned to understand how these words

Correct spelling	*Incorrect spelling*

evolved. They came into English from *eruditus*, the past participle
of a Latin verb meaning "to instruct," from the prefix *ex-* (out of)
and the adjective *rudis* (rude), a root that also came into English as
rude, of course, and **rudimentary**.

escape

eschew

escrow

esential	**essential**
eshew	**eschew**

esoteric, esotericism
> The roots of these words can be understood by anyone: the Late
> Latin *esotericus* came from a Greek adjective that derived from a
> word that meant "more within."

especially

espionage

espresso
> This word is pure Italian, from *caffè espresso*, which means
> "pressed out coffee." Although the adjective evolved from the
> same Latin verb that in English developed into **express**, it's
> spelled with an *s* because *x* is almost never used in Italian.

esprit de corps
> This expression is pure French, linking the words for "spirit" and
> "body" to mean "a feeling of togetherness, enthusiasm, and devo-
> tion to a common cause." All that in only three words!

esquire

essence, essential

essoteric	**esoteric***
essotericism	**esotericism***

esthetic, esthetics or aesthetic, aesthetics
> The spelling of these words is still changing. They came into
> English from German, from a Greek word, *aistheta* ("perceptible
> things").

Correct spelling	*Incorrect spelling*

et al.

This expression is an abbreviation of *et alii,* Latin for "and other people." A common error is to place a period after "et"; there isn't one because it's a word (and), not an abbreviation.

etamology	**etymology***
etaquette	**etiquette***

etc.

It's easier to remember how to spell this term if you keep in mind that it's an abbreviation of *et cetera,* Latin for "and other things."

et cetera

etequette	**etiquette***

ethanol

etimology	**etymology***

etiquette

This word is pure French, meaning "label." How did that word develop the meaning that we have in English? According to one explanation, this word and the related **ticket** derived from a Middle Dutch verb meaning "to stick," because notices were stuck up on posts, such as notices that set rules for behavior, thus establishing proper **etiquette**.

etymology

This word, which we've used throughout this book, has a Greek origin, as you might well guess from the ending, *–logy,* meaning "science." The first part of this word came from the adjective meaning "true," since **etymology** is the science of finding the truth or at least the true sense of words.

eucalyptus

eugenics

This word formed from the Greek words meaning "well" and born." That's also the meaning behind the name **Eugene**, "well born."

eulogize, eulogy

The root of these words is the Greek *eulogia,* "praise," from *eu* (good, well) and the suffix *–logia* (discourse, words).

Correct spelling	*Incorrect spelling*

eunuch

This word evolved through Latin and Middle English from a Greek word summarizing the purpose of the **eunuch**—"to keep" and "bed."

euphemism, euphemistic, euphemistically

We get these words from Greek, where *euphemismos* was based on an adjective meaning "using auspicious words," from *eu* (good) and *pheme* (speech).

euphoria, euphoric

euthanasia

This word is pure Greek—the prefix *eu-* means "good" and the core word comes from *thanatos*, meaning "death," a root word that has almost died in English, appearing only in such erudite words as **thanatopsis** and **thanatotic**.

eutopia	**utopia***
euvre	**oeuvre**

This word is used in English in the expression **hors d'oeuvre** and in referring to an artist's body of work. The word is pure French, for "work."

evocative, evoke

exacerbate

exadus	**exodus**

exaggerate

example

exasperate

This verb comes directly from Latin, from the past participle, *exasperatus*, of a verb that meant "to make very rough." The root, *asper* (rough), came into English in **asperity**.

exaust	**exhaust***
exausting	**exhausting***

exceed

Only three verbs in English end in *–ceed*. (The other two are **proceed** and **succeed**.)

excel, excellence, excellent

Correct spelling	*Incorrect spelling*

excentric	**eccentric***
excentricity	**eccentricity***

except/accept

To **except** is to exclude. To **accept** is to receive. The greatest source of confusion is the expression, "present company **excepted**."

excruciating

The origin of this word is crucial—or at least related to **crucial**. Both come from the Latin noun, *crux,* which is the **crux** of this explanation. **Excruciate** came from the past participle, *excruciatus,* of a Latin verb meaning "to crucify," which would involve intense physical pain.

exedus	**exodus**
exeed	**exceed***
exel	**excel**
exellence	**excellence**
exellent	**excellent**
exemplary	
exentric	**eccentric***
exentricity	**eccentricity***
exept	**except***

exercise

Exercise is one of 11 commonly misspelled verbs ending in *–ise*. The others are **advertise, advise, apprise, chastise, despise, devise, improvise, revise, supervise,** and **surprise**.

exhaust, exhausting

The silent *h* may cause a spelling problem. A friend remembers this *h* as representing the *h*eavy and *h*urried ex*h*aling and in*h*aling when she's ex*h*austed after *h*ard exercise.

exhilarate, exhilaration

The silent *h* in this word confuses some people—but not if they know that it comes from the same Latin and Greek root as **hilarious**, which originally meant merely "cheerful."

exhorbitant, exhorbitent	**exorbitant***
exhuberance	**exuberance***

Correct spelling	*Incorrect spelling*

Correct spelling	Incorrect spelling
exhuberant	**exuberant***
exilarate	**exhilarate***
exilaration	**exhilaration***

exist, existence, existent, existing

existential, existentialism, existentialist

exodus

exorbitant
> This word comes from Latin—*ex* (out of) and *orbita* (track), to mean something quite out of the routine. Remember to "X-out" the "h."

expectorant, expectorate
> **Expectorate** has an interesting origin: at least it's not what you might **expect**. It's from the past participle, *expectoratus*, of a Latin verb combining the prefix *ex-* (out of) and *pectus*, "chest," a word that came directly into English in **pectoral**. (The apparently similar **expect** also uses the prefix *ex-* but the root is *spectare*, "to watch," as in **expectation**.)

expediency, expedient, expeditious

expel, expelled, expulsion

expense, expensive

experience, experiential

explanation, explanatory

explicate

expresso	**espresso***
extacy, extasy	**ecstasy***

extemporaneous

extenuate, extenuating

extraneous
> This word came directly from a Latin adjective based on *extra*, "outside." That's simple enough. But that same adjective took a strange route to enter English in another way—passing through Old French and Middle English to emerge as **strange, stranger,** and **estrangement**.

Correct spelling	*Incorrect spelling*

extraordinary

extrapolate, extrapolation

extraterrestrial

extravert

extricate

This word is peculiar, because it's used only as a verb, while its exact antonym, **intricate,** is used only as an adjective. Both **extricate** and **intricate** come from a Latin root meaning "hindrances" or "perplexities."

extrinsic

extrordinary **extraordinary**

extrovert

exuberance, exuberant

We use these words to mean "full of enthusiasm or joy." But another, earlier meaning is "lavish" or "overflowing" or "abundant." The root is Latin, *uber*, "fertile."

Correct spelling *Incorrect spelling*

Incorrect	Correct
faccimile	**facsimile***
facea	**fascia***

facetious

facial

| *facil* | **facile*** |
| *facilatate* | **facilitate** |

facile
  This word is easy—literally. The root is *facilis*, Latin meaning "easy" or "doable."

facilitate, facilitator

| *facinate* | **fascinate** |

facsimile
  Facsimile (or **fax**) is a very modern use of this very old word, formed in Latin from two words, *fac simile* (make similar). The first word is part of many English words—such as **factotum**, **fact**, and **factor**—and the second word appears in **simile** and **similar**.

| *facsinate* | **fascinate** |

fair/fare
  Fair is an adjective or an adverb meaning good, moderate, honest, pleasant, and so forth, or a noun designating an exhibition or recreational event. **Fare** is a noun meaning a price for transportation, food, or entertainment or a verb meaning to get along or to manage.

| *fairwell* | **farewell** |

fairy/ferry
  A **fairy** is an imaginary being. A **ferry** is a boat.

| *falability* | **fallibility** |

| **Correct spelling** | *Incorrect spelling* |

falable	**fallible**
falacious	**fallacious**
falacy	**fallacy**

falafel
> This name for fried balls of ground spiced chickpeas and fava beans comes from Arabic. Will knowing that origin help you spell it? No.

fallability	**fallibility**
fallable	**fallible**

fallacious, fallacy

fallafel	**falafel***

fallible, fallibility

familiar
> This word has its roots in the Latin, *familia*, "family." That word evolved in two forms, **familiar** and **familial**, with slightly different meanings.

fanomenun	**phenomenon***
fantom	**phantom**

> This word derives from a Greek word meaning "to show." How does knowing its origin help you spell this word? Just remember that Greek had only one letter to represent the *f* sound—phi (*ph*).

fare/fair (see entry for **fair/fare**)

farewell

farmaceutical	**pharmaceutical**
farmacy	**pharmacy**

> This word comes from the Greek, *pharmakon*, "drug." Evidence of Greek origins is in the initial letters, since there was no *f* in Greek, only the letter *phi*.

farmaseutical	**pharmaceutical**
farmasy	**pharmacy***
fascea	**fascia***
fascetious	**facetious**

fascia
> This word for certain parts of a building is an Italian word derived

Correct spelling	*Incorrect spelling*

from the Latin word for "band" or "bandage" and related to the
word that gives us **fascism**.

fascinate

fascism, fascist, fascistic

These words are from the Italian word for "group," used to suggest that there is strength in unity.

fasetious	**facetious**
fashism	**fascism***
fasia	**fascia***
fasil	**facile***
fasilatate	**facilitate**
fasile	**facile***
fasilitate	**facilitate**
fasinate	**fascinate**
fassetious	**facetious**

fastidious

This word is closer in form than in meaning to its Latin roots: the
adjective *fastidiosus* was based on a noun meaning "loathing."

fategue	**fatigue**

fathom

fatigue

faximile	**facsimile***

Although we shorten this word as **fax**, you can remember the
spelling if you know that **facsimile** comes from two Latin words,
fac simile (make similar).

feasibility, feasible

This word comes from Latin, but through Old French and Middle
English, which makes it harder to recognize the Latin root, *facere*,
"to do.

feat/feet

A **feat** is an accomplishment. **Feet** are the things that allow you
to accomplish the **feat** of walking.

Correct spelling	*Incorrect spelling*

February
> People tend to pronounce this word incorrectly and spell it accordingly. Although the month follows January, the spelling does not. The word comes from a Latin festival related to the word that gives us **fever** and **febrile**.

fecetious	**facetious**

feet/feat (see entry for **feat/feet**)

feetal	**fetal**
feind	**fiend**
feindish	**fiendish**
felafel	**falafel***

feminism, feminist

fenomenun	**phenomenon***

ferry/fairy (see entry for **fairy/ferry**)

fescetious	**facetious**

fester

festoon

fetaccini	**fettuccine/ fettuccini***

fetal

fettuccine/fettuccini
> This word comes from Italian, where it's spelled **fettuccine**, the plural of *fettuccina*, which means "narrow ribbon" or "very thin slice." Both spellings are used in English.

fetus

fiancé, fiancée
> These words are pure French, even to the two endings, –é (masculine) and –ée (feminine). The words are forms of a verb that evolved from the Latin, *fidare*, "to trust."

fiasco
> This word is Italian, closely related to **flask**. When glassmakers in Italy blew glass that was too flawed for finer purposes, they put

Correct spelling	*Incorrect spelling*

the "mistake" aside to recycle into flasks, so the word **fiasco** became synonymous with failure.

fidelity

fiduciary

field

fiend

fiery

This word shows the earlier form of the word **fire**—a Middle English word, *fier*.

filafel	**falafel***

filament

filanderer	**philanderer***
filandering	**philandering***
filanthopic	**philanthropic**
filanthropy	**philanthropy**

finagle

finance, financial, financier

These basic terms of our financial world developed in an odd way. The Middle English word meaning "money supply" came from an Old French verb, *finer*, "to pay off," from a Latin root, *finis*, "end," because **finance** was originally a payment to put an end to a business affair. Whew! So, when you pay a **fine** that depletes your **finances**, just remember that you're keeping it all in the same linguistic family.

finesse

fir/fur

A **fir** is a type of pine tree. **Fur** is the hairy coat of a mammal.

fisacal, fisakal, fisical, fisikal	**physical**
fisishun	**physician**

flabbergasted

flaccid

flagellate, flagellation

| **Correct spelling** | *Incorrect spelling* |

flagrant

This word means "extremely conspicuous" or "shocking," but the meaning was originally much more concrete. The word comes from the Latin verb, *flagrare*, "to burn." We find forms of this root in **conflagration** and the legal term *flagrante delicto*, literally "while the crime is blazing."

flail

flack/flak

Flack is slang for "press agent." **Flak** is a shortened form of the German word for antiaircraft artillery—*Fliegerabwehrkanone*. (It's easy to see why this word was shortened!)

flamboyant

flatulence, flatulent

flaunt/flout

These two words are not really homophones, but close enough that people sometimes confuse them. To **flaunt** is to show off something, while to **flout** is to ignore or scoff at.

fleece

flem	**phlegm***
flese	**fleece**

flexibility, flexible

floor

flore	**floor**
floresent	**fluorescent***
florine	**fluorine**

flour/flower

Flour is a powdered form of milled grain. A **flower** is a plant with blossoms. That may seem like a simple case of homophones that are easily distinguished. In truth, they're much further together in meaning than we might expect. **Flower** grew out of the Middle English *flour*, which came from the Latin *flos, floris*. That's why we have the varied forms **flowering**, **flourishing**, and **floriferous**.

flourescent	**fluorescent***

Correct spelling	*Incorrect spelling*

flout/flaunt (see entry for **flaunt/flout**)

flower/flour (see entry for **flour/flower**)

flunky

fluorescent

>The first part of this word comes from a mineral named after the Latin word that gives us **flux** and **fluid** and **fluent**. So, even though we don't pronounce the *u* in **fluorescent**, we still retain it in the spelling.

fluorine

focaccia

>This recent addition to English is an Italian word for a flat bread typically seasoned with herbs and olive oil. It comes from the Latin word *focus* (hearth).

for/fore/four

>**For** is a preposition with various meanings or a conjunction synonymous with "because." **Fore** is an adjective, an adverb, a noun, and a prefix, generally referring to the front or forward. **Four** is a number.

foran   **foreign**

fore/for/four (see entry for **for/fore/four**)

foreclose, foreclosure

forefeit   **forfeit**

forego/forgo

>**Forgo** is to go without, so think of it as the verb that goes without the e. **Forego** is to *go* be**fore**.

forehead

foreign, foreigner

>These words come from a Latin root, *foras*, meaning "outside." Compare the words that developed from the Latin synonym, *extra*—**extraneous** and, through French, **strange** and **stranger**.

foreword/forward

>**Foreword** is the **words** in a book be**fore** the main text. **Forward** is the opposite of **backward**, related to **inward** and **outward**—all denoting direction or location.

| **Correct spelling** | *Incorrect spelling* |

forfeit

forgo/forego (see entry for **forego/forgo**)

foriegn   **foreign***

formaldehyde

formally/formerly

> These two words are not true homophones, but they're sometimes confused. **Formally** refers to doing something in an official or established way, while **formerly** indicates something past.

formeldahyde, formeldehyde   **formaldehyde**

formerly/formally (see entry for **formally/formerly**)

forth/fourth

> **Forth** is a synonym for **forward**. **Fourth** is a ranking between third and fifth.

fortieth

fortuitous

> The root of this word is the Latin, *fors*, "chance." That root also developed into **fortunate**.

forty

forward/foreword (see entry for **foreword/forward**)

fotograph   **photograph***

fotographer   **photographer***

fotography   **photography***

four/for/fore (see entry for **for/fore/four**)

fourth/forth (see entry for **forth/fourth**)

fourty   **forty**

> Why is it **four** and **fourteen**, but **forty** without the *u*? Good question! But you can remember this spelling if you just think of the zero in 40 as meaning no *u* in **forty**.

foyer

> This elegant word for "lobby" or "entrance hall" we get straight from French, which is why we pronounce it in various ways. The meaning in French is "hearth," from the Latin word, *focus*. Since

---

Correct spelling   *Incorrect spelling*

the hearth was the center of the home, the word **focus** acquired the meaning of "center."

fragile, fragility

frail

Frail comes from the same Latin adjective as **fragile** (*fragilis*). Since words tend to be fragile tools, they change with usage, which explains how **frail** lost more of its original form than its sibling **fragile** and how its meaning evolved.

frame

franetic   **frenetic***

frantic, frantically

These words come from a Greek term for a brain disease, which also is the root of **frenzy** and **frenetic**.

frappé or **frappe**

frate   **freight**

frater   **freighter**

frazzle

freak, freakish, freaky

These words are freaks in that their origin remains unknown.

freight, freighter

freind   **friend**

frenetic

This word and **frenzy** and **frantic** come from a Greek term for a brain disease.

frenzy

fresco

This word comes straight from Italian, from the Germanic root that develops into **fresh**. We've also borrowed the expression *alfresco*, meaning "in the fresh air" or "outdoors."

friend, friendliness, friendly

fright, frighten, frightened

fritter

This word has two meaning and two origins. The name of the

food comes through Old French and Middle English from the Latin verb for "to fry." The verb comes from a word that meant "fragment," with an earlier meaning, now rare, of "to break into bits," which is how the meaning developed of "squandering little by little."

frivolity, frivolous

frumpy

fuchsia

This word is easier to spell if you know that the plant and thus the color were named after Leonard Fuchs, a 16th-century German botanist.

fufill **fulfill***

fugitive

fulfill

Why do we use only one *l* when the word **full** is compounded in **fulfill**? Because that was the spelling in Old English—which we still use as a suffix in the many words such as **awful** and **tea-spoonful** and **roomful**, to mention just a few.

funal **funnel**

function, functional, functionality

funel **funnel**

funeral

funky

funnel

funomenun **phenomenon***

fur/fir (see entry for **fir/fur**)

furnace

fuschia **fuchsia***

fusetious **facetious**

Correct spelling *Incorrect spelling*

gaily

    This adverb formed from **gay** follows the same rule as **day** becoming **daily.**

galan	**gallon**
galant	**gallant***
galary	**gallery**

galaxy

    This word comes through space and time from the Greek *galaxias,* "milky." Even now, **galaxy** (generally capitalized) can mean Milky Way.

galen	**gallon**
galery	**gallery**
galiant	**gallant***
Galic	**Gallic***

gall

gallant

    This adjective, with its several pronunciations, came into English from French, from a verb derived from a Germanic word, *gale,* meaning "to rejoice," a root that also evolved into **regale** and (through Italian and Old Spanish) **gala.**

gallary	**gallery**
gallaxy	**galaxy**
gallen	**gallon**
gallery	
galliant	**gallant***

Correct spelling	*Incorrect spelling*

Gallic

This adjective referring to France (as in **Gallic** wit or **Gallic** charm) comes from the Latin *Gallicus,* based on the word that the Romans used to refer to the area that is now France, *Gallia.*

gallon

gallop

gambit

Gambit comes from an Italian word for "leg." The word was originally used for an opening move in chess (the first leg of a journey to victory?), then for any maneuver or strategy. Don't confuse **gambit** with **gamut**.

gamut

Gamut is a Middle English term for the musical scale, a term we now use to mean an entire range of things—choices, emotions, and so forth. Don't confuse **gamut** with **gambit**.

Gantt

This term for a horizontal bar chart that displays the time relationships among tasks in a project is named after Henry L. Gantt (1861-1919) who invented the chart as a way to schedule work crews across a series of tasks.

garage

garalous, garalus	**garrulous**
garantee	**guarantee***
garelous	**garrulous**

gargantuan

This word comes from the name of a giant character created by the 16th century French author, François Rabelais.

garrage	**garage**

garrulous

gas, gaseous, gases (or gasses)

gase	**gaze**
gasha	**geisha***

gasoline

Correct spelling	*Incorrect spelling*

gauche

This French word shows the traditional bias against left-handed people. In French it means "left," but the origin was a verb meaning "to turn aside," of Germanic origin. Since in battle a soldier would turn aside a blow with his shield, generally held with the left hand, the association was natural.

gaudy

This adjective derives from a Middle English word, *gaude*, meaning "trinket."

gauge

gaunt

gauntlet

This word has two uses, from two distinct origins. When we talk about "throwing down the **gauntlet**," to issue a challenge, we're using a word from Old French that meant "glove." But when we talk of "running the **gauntlet**," we're using a word that comes from two Swedish words meaning "lane" and "course," for a punishment in which someone was forced to run between two lines of people armed with sticks to beat him. That punishment has come to denote any ordeal or severe trial.

gauze

gawdy	**gaudy***
gawze	**gauze**
gayly	**gaily***

gaze

gear

geisha

This word has acquired connotations that obscure the original meaning. The word is Japanese, of course, combining *gei*, "art," and *sha*, "person."

gelatin, gelatinous

genacide	**genocide***
genaric	**generic***

| **Correct spelling** | *Incorrect spelling* |

genaside   **genocide***

genealogical, genealogist, genealogy

We can trace the "blood lines" of these words back through Old French and Latin to Greek, from *genea* (family) and *–logia* (science or study). This word is easy to spell if you think of the troublesome vowel in the center as *a* for **ancestor**.

general, generalize, generally

generic

This word and **general** come from the Latin word, *genus*, meaning "kind" or "type." We've borrowed this root directly for the scientific **genus**, while **general** came from the Latin *generalis* (of the kind or typical) and **generic** developed through French.

genial

genius

gennacidal   **genocidal***

gennacide   **genocide***

genneric   **generic***

genocidal, genocide

These words are easy to spell if you remember the mixed root: Greek *genos* (race) and Latin *–cide* (killing), as in **homicide, suicide, pesticide, insecticide,** and **herbicide**.

gesture

giddy

giesha   **geisha***

gigolo

gingham

The name for this fabric is Malay, *ginggang*, meaning "striped."

giraffe

giro

This word used in Europe for an authorized direct transfer of bank funds is related to the circulation of currency and bank transfers. The word comes from the Latin root as **gyrate** and **gyroscope**, but it came through Italian, which has no *y*.

| **Correct spelling** | *Incorrect spelling* |

gist

glacial, glacier

glaze

glean

> To **glean** is "to gather bit by bit," from a Middle English verb that came through Old French from Latin. The earlier meaning of **glean** was agricultural, "to gather from a field what's left behind by harvesters."

glitch

gloss, glossary

> These words come from Latin, *glossa*, meaning "a word requiring an explanation," from Greek, where *glossa* meant "tongue" and, figuratively, "language." But when we use the expression "**gloss** over" or the word **glossy**, the words are from a Germanic or Scandinavian source meaning "sheen," perhaps related to **glass** and **glare** (sheet or surface of ice).

gluteus

goal

gonorrhea

gorgeous

gormay, gormet   **gourmet***

gospel

gost   **ghost**

gourmet

> The pronunciation marks this word as French; the meaning in Old French was "a wine merchant's steward," who would certainly be expected to be an expert in fine dining. Related to this word is **gourmand**, also French, a word that came into Middle English as "glutton" from Old French.

goverment   **government**

governer   **governor**

government, governmental

governor

Correct spelling	*Incorrect spelling*

grace, graceful, gracious

graf   **graph**

graffiti, graffito

This word is Italian, meaning "something scratched" (on a wall). The *−i* ending marks the plural, while the *−o* ending is singular.

grafic   **graphic**

grammar

It's easier to remember the *−a−* in the second syllable if you think of the adjective form, **grammatical**.

grandeur

The *−eur* ending (such as we find in **amateur, chauffeur, connoisseur,** and **entrepreneur**) marks this word as a French noun. It retains the original meaning of the adjective **grand** as "great."

graph, graphic

graphiti   **graffiti***

gratuitous

gratuity

The fancy word for "tip" came through Old French from Latin, *gratia,* meaning "favor," based on the adjective for "pleasing" that developed into such words as **graceful** and **gracious**. So, be gracious and leave a gratuity!

grease, greasy

greavance   **grievance***

greave   **grieve***

greavous   **grievous***

greazy   **greasy**

gregarious

This word came from a Latin root, *grex,* meaning "a flock or herd." The original meaning was "belonging to a herd or flock." From there it came to mean sociable. That same root is also found in **congregation, segregate, aggregate,** and **egregious**.

grievance, grieve, grievous

The old principle of "*i* before *e* except after *c*" works for **grieve** and related words.

Correct spelling   *Incorrect spelling*

grommet

grotesque

gruff

Although this word rhymes with two words often associated with it, **rough** and **tough**, the spelling of the shared sound is different. That's because **gruff** came into English in the 18th century from Dutch, while **rough** and **tough** developed in Middle English from Old English roots, with the ending forming along the same phonetic lines as the final sound of **laugh** and **enough**. To remember the spelling of **gruff**, think of another word that's often associated with being **gruff—bluff**.

guage   **gauge/gage**

The preferred spelling is **gauge**, but **gage** is acceptable.

guarantee

The *u* that we don't pronounce in **guarantee** reveals that the word came to us from German through French. The related word **warranty** came into English directly; however, since French didn't have a *w*, the sound represented by the *w* in German became *gu* in French, which gave us **guarantee**. Compare the doublets **guile** and **wiles** and **guardian** and **warden**.

gubernatorial

This word comes from the same Latin root, *gubernator*, as **governor**. However, **gubernatorial** entered into English relatively recently (1734), while **governor** has been around since the 14th century and has evolved more from the Latin root.

guidance

gumbo

This word and the thick soup come from a Louisiana French word that originated in Africa, in Bantu.

guverment	**government**
guvernatorial	**gubernatorial***
guvernment	**government**

gyrate

gyro

This word for a pita sandwich is modern Greek, from the word for "turn" or "circle," as in **gyroscope** or **gyrate**.

Correct spelling	*Incorrect spelling*

habeas corpus
This legal term for a writ is Latin, meaning "you should have the body"—the opening words of the writ.

hackneyed
This term for words that have become trite or worn out through overuse comes from a breed of horse raised in Hackney, a borough of England. The carriage or coach pulled by the horses was also called a hackney, which was the origin of our use of **hack** for a taxicab and then for the driver and eventually for anybody who worked for hire, especially writers. When a horse or a word is used too often, either will become tired and lose its vitality.

haggard

hail/hale
Hail is a verb meaning to greet someone or signal for a taxi and it's a noun and a verb for icy precipitation or a figurative shower. **Hale** is a synonym of healthy, usually used only in the expression "**hale** and hearty."

hairbrained	**harebrained***
halatosis	**halitosis**

hale/hail (see entry for **hail/hale**)

halitosis

hallowed

Halloween

hallucinate, hallucination, hallucinatory

hallucinogen, hallucinogenic

Correct spelling   *Incorrect spelling*

handkerchief

hangar/hanger

Think of **hangar** as containing the first syllable of *garage*: it's where aircraft are parked. The **hanger** is something that hangs, so the ending *–er* is natural.

hankercheif, hankerchief   **handkerchief**

Our pronunciation of this word makes the spelling more difficult. It's a **kerchief** used by the **hand**. What's a **kerchief**? Something that covers the head—but this word uses a form of an Old French word for "cover" (*ker-* here but *cur-* in **curfew**, "cover fire") and the Old French word for "head," which we still have in **chief**.

hanous   **heinous***

haracy   **heresy**

harakiri or **hara-kiri**

We've changed the pronunciation of this Japanese word for "ritual suicide," a word that means literally "belly cutting."

harangue

The *–ngue* ending occurs only in **harangue, tongue,** and **meringue**—all words from the French.

harass, harassment

Harass comes from French, from an Old French verb meaning "to set a dog on." (The original meaning also comes to us in such verbs as "to hound" or "to dog" someone.) From those origins the word evolved to mean "irritate" or "torment persistently."

harasy   **heresy**

harebrained

This word comes from the belief that the rabbit (**hare**) lacks intelligence.

harras   **harass***

harrasment   **harassment***

harrass   **harass***

harrassment   **harassment***

Correct spelling   *Incorrect spelling*

harrasy   **heresy**

hasta la vista

This phrase, made famous by an action movie, is Spanish for "goodbye."

haughty

haute

This word is French, meaning "high" or "refined," and it's usually used with *cuisine* (cooking) or *couture* (fashion). The *h* is not pronounced and the *–au-* is pronounced as a long *o*, so this word sounds like the English *oat*.

heal/heel

Heal is to restore to *health*. **Heel** is a part of a foot, shoe, or sock or to follow at someone's heels.

health, healthy

heel/heal (see entry for **heal/heel**)

height, heighten

These words are easy to spell if you remember that they contain the word **eight**—and certainly anybody eight feet tall has **height**.

heighth   **height**

Although the nouns for the three dimensions **wide, long**, and **high** should follow a certain logic, it's **width** and **length** with *–th*, but **height** with just a *–t*.

heinous

We rarely use this adjective any more, except in the expression "**heinous** crime." It came into Middle English from an Old French word for "hateful," of Germanic origin.

heir, heiress

Although a **heritage** is something enjoyed by an **heir**, that word is not found in **heritage, hereditary, inherit,** or **inheritance**. Why not? Because **heir** evolved from the Latin root, *heres*, through French, so the word changed more than the other words, which stayed closer to their Latin root.

heiroglyphics   **hieroglyphics***

Correct spelling   *Incorrect spelling*

helicopter

helth	**health**
helthy	**healthy**
hemarage	**hemorrhage***
hemaroid	**hemorrhoid**

hematoma

hemerage	**hemorrhage***
hemmeroid	**hemorrhoid**

hemorrhage

This word came through Old French and Latin from a Greek word that combined the words for "blood" and "to break."

hemorrhoid

hepatitis

herasy	**heresy**
heratage	**heritage**
heratic	**heretic**

herbicide

Herculean

heard/herd

Heard is the past tense of hear. **Herd** is a group of grazing animals.

herd/heard (see entry for **heard/herd**)

herecy	**heresy**

hereditary

heresy, heretic, heretical

hering	**herring**
herisy	**heresy**

heritage

heritic	**heretic**

hero, heroes

The first **hero** was Greek, from the word *heros*.

Correct spelling	*Incorrect spelling*

heroic

heroin/heroine

>**Heroin** without an –e is a drug, named for the feeling of power experienced while using the drug. **Heroine** with an –e is the female version of **hero,** from the Greek word *heroine.*

heroine/heroin (see entry for **heroin/heroine**)

herpes

herresy   **heresy**

hersuit   **hirsute**

>This fancy word for "hairy" or "shaggy" came into English in the 17th century straight from the Latin word *hirsutus.*

hi/high

>**Hi** is a greeting. It's also a shortened form of **high** that should be used only when space requires it. **High** is the opposite of low.

hiccup

>The spelling of this word derived from the sound. A variant spelling, **hiccough,** may have been influenced by the spelling of **cough,** which is of Middle English origin.

hick

>This word was once a nickname for Richard.

hidralic, hidraulic   **hydraulic**

hierarchical, hierarchy

>We get these words from the ancient Greeks, from a word that meant "rule of a high priest."

hieroglyphics

>This word comes through Latin from a Greek word combining the words for "sacred" and "carving." We find the root word for "sacred" in **hierarchy.** The word for "carving" survives in **glyph**—the word for a symbol that conveys information without words, such as pictures on street signs and bathroom doors.

higeine, higene   **hygiene**

high/hi (see entry for **hi/high**)

higherarchical   **hierarchical***

Correct spelling   *Incorrect spelling*

higherarchy	**hierarchy***
highth	**height**

Although this noun comes from the adjective **high**, it contains an —e-, just as the noun **neighbor** contains an —e- but not the archaic related adjective **nigh**.

highway

higiene, higine	**hygiene**

hinder, hindrance

hipacritical	**hypocritical**
hipadermic	**hypodermic***
hipe	**hype**

Hype is the use of **hyperbole**.

hiperbole	**hyperbole**
hiperbolic	**hyperbolic**
hipnatize, hipnetize, hipnotize	**hypnotize**
hipocondria	**hypochondria***
hipocondriac	**hypochondriac***
hipocrasy, hipocrisy	**hypocrisy**
hipocrite	**hypocrite**
hipocritical	**hypocritical**
hipodermic	**hypodermic***
hipopotamus	**hippopotamus**
hipotenuse	**hypotenuse**
hipothermia	**hypothermia**
hipothesis	**hypothesis***
hipothetical	**hypothetical***

hippo

hippocrasy	**hypocrisy**
hippocrite	**hypocrite**
hippocritical	**hypocritical**

hippopotamus

Correct spelling	*Incorrect spelling*

Incorrect spelling	Correct spelling
hiroglyphics	**hieroglyphics***
hirsute	
histerectomy	**hysterectomy***
histeria	**hysteria***
histerical	**hysterical***
histerics	**hysterics***

histrionics

We use this term for "exaggerated emotional behavior calculated for effect," but the original meaning of the word was neutral. It came into Latin from an Etruscan root and simply meant "pertaining to an actor."

hiway	**highway**

hoarse/horse

Hoarse means "having a low, harsh, or husky voice." A **horse** is an animal.

hoary

This word for "gray or white with age" or "ancient" derives from **hoar**, a synonym for **hoarfrost**.

hoax

The origin of this word is uncertain, although it may come from *hocus*, a pseudo Latin word used in **hocus-pocus**, a term that's also of uncertain origin.

hodgepodge

This word for a mixture of dissimilar items came into Middle English from an Old French word for a stew.

hole/whole

A **hole** is a cavity or an opening and **whole** means "complete" or "a complete entity."

holistic

holocaust

This word combines the Greek words *holo-* (whole, entire) and *–caust*, from the word for "to burn," a root also found in **caustic** and (slightly modified) **cauterize**.

hologram

Correct spelling	*Incorrect spelling*

homacide	**homicide**

homage

This word for a special honor bestowed on someone comes from a medieval feudal relationship. A friend suggests a mnemonic for remembering the spelling: *h*onor *o*r *m*erit *a*nd *g*eneral *e*steem. Whatever works!

homagenize	**homogenize**
homaside	**homicide**

home/hone

These two are not true homophones, but we sometimes confuse them in certain uses, particularly "**home** in on" (to get closer to something, as in "**homing** pigeons") and "to **hone** skills" (to sharpen).

homeopathic, homeopathy

These words for a medical treatment or approach derive through Latin from Greek words meaning "similar" and "suffering."

homeostasis

homicide

hommage	**homage***
hommicide	**homicide**
homogeanize	**homogenize**

homogeneity

homogeneous or **homogenous**

homogenization, homogenize

hone/home (see entry for **home/hone**)

honor, honorable

hoodwink

hooligan

This word is of unknown origin, although it probably came from the name of a 19th-century hoodlum in London, Patrick Hooligan.

hopeful

hoping

This is a form of the verb **hope**. The formation follows the rule: if the verb ends in an –e, drop the –e and add –*ing*. If you mean **hop**, it's **hopping**.

Correct spelling	*Incorrect spelling*

hopping

This is a form of the verb **hop**. The formation follows the rule: if the verb ends in a consonant, double the consonant and add –ing. If you mean **hope**, it's **hoping**.

Correct	Incorrect
horable	**horrible**
horafy	**horrify**
horascope	**horoscope***
hore	**whore**
horible	**horrible**
horify	**horrify**
horor	**horror**

horoscope

This word goes back to the Ancients, to the Greek *horoscopus*, a combination of the words for "hour" and "observer." Only true believers now care about the hour of birth.

horrible

horrify, horrifying

horror

horroscope	**horoscope***
horry	**hoary***

hors d'oeuvre

The spelling of this French term may make more sense if you understand how it derived: *hors* (out), *d'* (of), and *oeuvre* (work). The last word, **oeuvre**, has been borrowed into English for a work of art or the entire production of an artist.

horse/hoarse (see entry for **hoarse/horse**)

hory	**hoary***

hospitable

hospitality

hubris

humerus/humorous

Humerus is the spelling you want if you mean the long bone

Correct spelling   *Incorrect spelling*

that ends at the elbow and the "funny bone," where a sharp blow can cause a sensation that is really not **humorous**. If you mean funny, it's **humorous**.

humiliate, humiliation, humility

humor

humorous/humerus (see entry for **humerus/humorous**)

hurpes   **herpes**

hurricane

This word comes out of the Caribbean, through Spanish. To remember the spelling, just think of it as a storm that *hurri*es through the sugar *cane*.

hursute   **hirsute***

hydraulic

hydroplane

hygiene, hygienic

hypadermic   **hypodermic**

hype

hyperbole, hyperbolic

hypnotism, hypnotist, hypnotize

hypochondria, hypochondriac

These words come from the Greek word for "abdomen"—*hypo-* (under) and *–chondria* (cartilage [of the sternum])—a natural location for an imaginary sickness.

hypocrisy, hypocrite, hypocritical

hypodermic

The two pieces of this word are Greek for "under" or "beneath" and "skin." Both roots are used in many English words, such as **hypothermia** and **dermatology**, which should help with the spelling.

hypotenuse

hypothermia

Correct spelling   *Incorrect spelling*

hypothesis, hypothetical

These words are Greek, from a word meaning "to suppose," formed from the words *hypo* (beneath or under) and *tithenai* (to place). The word **suppose** has the same meaning, but from Latin words, *sub* (under or beneath) and *ponere* (to place).

hyppocrisy	**hypocrisy**
hyppocrite	**hypocrite**
hyppocritical	**hypocritical**
hyrogliphics	**hieroglyphics***

hysterectomy

hysteria, hysterical, hysterics

These words come from the Greek word that evolved into **uterus**, a root that we also find in **hysterectomy**. The ancients believed that **hysteria** was due to disturbances in the womb.

hystrionics	**histrionics***

Correct spelling   *Incorrect spelling*

ibuprofen

icicle

icon

This word has recently been appropriated for computer use, but it's an old term for any image, particularly sacred. It comes through Latin from a Greek word, *eikon*, meaning "likeness" or "image."

iconoclasm, iconoclast, iconoclastic

Iconoclasm, the attacking of traditional or popular practices or beliefs, has its roots in Greek, with the original meaning being "to break images."

iconography

idalize   **idolize**

ideal, idealism, idealist, idealistic

identification, identify

ideological, ideology

idiosyncracy   **idiosyncrasy**

This word is misspelled when people think of the ending of such words as **democracy**. But this word comes from a Greek word, *syncrasis*, which means mixing together of elements. The first part of the word comes from the same root as **idiot**.

idiosyncratic

idle/idol

Think of the *–le* ending of **idle** as standing for "*less* energy," which is what you use when you're **idle**, and think of the *–o–* in the word **idol** as standing for "object" that is worshipped.

| Correct spelling | *Incorrect spelling* |

idol/idle (see entry for **idle/idol**)

idolize

i.e.
> This expression is hard to misspell, but easy to misuse. It's an abbreviation of *id est,* Latin for "that is (to say)." Remember to put a period after each letter.

ignision	**ignition**

ignite

ignition

ignoble

ignominious, ignominy
> These words to describe shameful or dishonorable actions come from Latin, *ignominia,* combing the words for "not" and "name" or "reputation."

ignoramus
> This word is pure Latin for "we do not know."

ignorance, ignorant

ikon	**icon***
ikonography	**iconography**
iland	**island***
ilegitamate	**illegitimate**
ilicet, ilicit, ilisit	**illicit**
iliterate	**illiterate**

ilk
> We got this word from an Old English word meaning "same."

illegitimate

illicit/elicit (see entry for **elicit/illicit**)

illiterate

illogical

illude	**elude, elusive**

illuminate

illusion/allusion (see entry for **allusion/illusion**)
illusory

Incorrect spelling	Correct spelling
ilogical	**illogical**
ilude, ilusive	**elude, elusive**
ilumenate, iluminate	**illuminate**
ilusion	**illusion**

imaginary, imagination, imagine
imbibe
> This word dates back to a Latin verb, *imbibere*, "to drink in," from a root that passes through Old French and Middle English to emerge as **beverage**. The words **bib** (noun and verb) and **bibulous** seem to derive from the same Latin root.

imbroglio
> The pronunciation of this word reveals its Italian origin. But it seems to have come into Italian from a French word meaning "to confuse"—which is what the word may do.

Incorrect spelling	Correct spelling
imediate	**immediate**
iminent	**imminent**

immediate, immediately
> These words come from a Latin root meaning roughly "with nothing in the middle." We find the prefix *im-* in numerous words and the root in such words as **medium, media, mediator**, and **intermediary**.

immense
> Only a few words end in *–ense*: **immense** and **defense, expense, offense**, and **pretense**.

imminent/eminent, imminence/eminence (see entry for **eminent/imminent, eminence/imminence**)
immune, immunity
impartial, impartiality

Incorrect spelling	Correct spelling
impasable	**impassable**
impass	**impasse**

> That silent final *–e* marks this borrowing from French, similar in form to **finesse** and **en masse**.

Correct spelling	Incorrect spelling

impassable

impasse

impeach

This word so prominent in the news recently comes down through the centuries from a Latin verb, *impedicare*, meaning "to entangle," from *pedica*, "fetter." (We treat politicians just as the Romans treated their horses!) The root word is related to **impede** and **impediment**.

impeccable

This word (flawless, perfect) is the opposite (*im-*) of **peccable** (liable to sin), a word that's rarely used now, from a Latin root that's also found in **peccadillo** (little sin or slight fault).

imperial, imperious

impersonate, impersonation

impetuosity, impetuous

These words leap into English from Latin, from the root *impetus*, which originally meant "attack." Our direct borrowing of **impetus** has only the attenuated meaning of "impelling force," "impulse," or "stimulus."

impetus

implement

importune

impostor

This word as the same Latin root as **impose**: an **impostor** puts on an identity and **imposes** it on others.

impower	**empower**

impromptu

impunity

imune	**immune**
imunity	**immunity**
inabition	**inhibition**

inadvertent

A friend remembers the troublesome final syllable of this word by

Correct spelling	*Incorrect spelling*

thinking, "I was **inadvertent** when I pitched the **tent** near the wasp nest."

inane, inanity

Inanity has been a human flaw through the ages. The root of these words is the Latin adjective, *inanis*, meaning "empty," hence our use of the word to mean "empty of substance and/or sense."

inate	**innate***

inaugural, inaugurate, inauguration

inavate	**innovate**
inavation	**innovation**
inavertant, inavertent	**inadvertent***

incandescent

incarnate, incarnation

incedently	**incidentally***

incentive

incessant

incident, incidentally

These words come almost straight from Latin, from *incidens*, the present participle of a verb meaning "to happen," which has an interesting root in the verb "to fall."

incinuate	**insinuate***
incipid	**insipid***

incipient

This word began to exist in the past participle of a Latin verb, *incipiens*, "beginning." That verb was the root of a noun, *inceptio*, that came straight into English as **inception**.

incisive

incite/insight

Incite is a verb meaning to provoke. **Insight** is a noun derived from "seeing into" a situation or a person.

incognito

The identity of this word is not well disguised: it's an Italian word

Correct spelling	*Incorrect spelling*

coming from Latin, *incognitus*, meaning "not known." Another form of this Latin adjective is found in the expression **terra incognita**—literally "unknown land," figuratively "new territory." So now you know!

incoherent

This word is the negative (*in-*) of coherent, which comes from Latin, from two core words stuck together, "together" and "to stick" or "to cling." From the Latin root verb we also get **adhere**, **inherent**, and **hesitate**.

incompatible

incompetent

This word is easy to spell if you remember that it's hard to **compete** successfully if you're **incompetent**.

inconsistency, inconsistent

incontinence, incontinent

incorrigibility, incorrigible

These words come from a Latin adjective, *incorrigibilis*, that derived from the verb *corrigere*, "to correct." The past participle of that verb, *correctum*, also came into English.

incredible

incredulous

increment, incremental

These words are almost pure Latin, from *incrementum*, the past participle of the verb that also came into as **increase** and **crescent**.

Incorrect spelling	Correct spelling
indeavor	**endeavor**
indemic	**endemic***
independence, independent	
indevor	**endeavor**
indict, indictment	
indigeanous	**indigenous**
indigence, indigent	

Correct spelling	*Incorrect spelling*

indigenous

indigo

This word is Spanish, from a Latin word that came from a Greek term, *indikon pharmakon*, that meant "Indian dye." So, when we refer to the color **indigo**, we're actually naming the source of the pigment.

indispensable

indubitable, indubitably

The core of this pair of words is *dubitare*, Latin for "to doubt." That verb evolved through Old French and Middle English into **doubt**. So now we have **indubitably** and **undoubtedly**, synonyms that took different routes from the same source.

inebriated

inedible

ineffable

This word means "indescribable," but we can certainly explain it. It comes from Latin, *effabilis*, "that can be uttered," from the verb meaning "to speak out."

inept, ineptitude

Hidden in this word is another. **Inept** came from the same Latin adjective, *aptus*, as **apt**. Siblings separated at birth, they no longer share the same vowel and have opposite meanings.

inerest   **interest***

inevitable

inexcusable

infallibility, infallible

infatuate, infatuation

These words have the same root as **fatuous**—the Latin adjective, *fatuus*, "foolish."

infinite

infinitesimal

infinity

| **Correct spelling** | *Incorrect spelling* |

Correct spelling	Incorrect spelling
inflamable	**inflammable**
inflamation	**inflammation**
inflamatory	**inflammatory**

inflammable

inflammation

inflammatory

ingenious

Although someone who's **ingenious** may be considered a **genius**, the two similar words have different origins. **Ingenious** comes from the Latin *ingenium*, meaning "inborn talent." **Genius** is pure Latin, a word meaning "guardian spirit," a force that animates and inspires.

ingenue

ingenuity

ingenuous

This is a completely different word from **ingenious**. **Ingenuous** means innocent. A related word is **ingénue**.

inhalant, inhalation, inhale

The very breath of these words comes from the same root as **halitosis**—the Latin verb, *halere*, meaning "to breathe."

inheirent	**inherent**
inheirit	**inherit**

inherent

inherit

inherrent	**inherent**

inhibition

inimacy	**intimacy***
inimate	**intimate***

initial, initially

initiate, initiative

innacent	**innocent***

Correct spelling	*Incorrect spelling*

innane	**inane***
innasent	**innocent***

innate

    This word comes from Latin, *in-* (in) and *natus* (born in). You can think of **innate** characteristics as being *in nat*ure.

innaugural	**inaugural**
innaugurate	**inaugurate**
innauguration	**inauguration**
innebriated	**inebriated**
innedable, innedible	**inedible**
innerest	**interest***
innibition	**inhibition**
innimacy	**intimacy***
innimate	**intimate***
innitial	**initial**
innitiate	**initiate**
innitiative	**initiative**

innocent

    Being **innocent** means not causing harm. This word is a Latin combination of *in-* (not) and *nocens* (causing harm).

innoculate	**inoculate**
innoculation	**inoculation**

innocuous

    It's easier to remember the double *n* if you know that this word is Latin, *in-* (not) and *nocuus* (harmful), a root we also find hidden in **noxious**.

innorganic	**inorganic**

innovate, innovation, innovative

innuendo, innuendoes

    This noun is a borrowing of a Latin verb form, *innuendo*, which comes from a verb meaning "to give a nod."

innumerable

Correct spelling	*Incorrect spelling*

innundate	**inundate***
inoccuous	**innocuous***
inocent	**innocent***

inoculate, inoculation

You'll never again have trouble spelling this word, once you know the origin. It's in the past participle, *inoculatus*, of a Latin verb that meant "to graft a scion," from the prefix *in-* (in) and the base noun *oculus*, here meaning "a bud," but usually meaning "an eye."

inocuous	**innocuous***
inovate	**innovate**
inovation	**innovation**

inquisition, inquisitive

insalar	**insular***
insalarity	**insularity***
insalate	**insulate**
insalation	**insulation**
insalin	**insulin**

insane, insanity

inscrutable

The Latin root, *scrutabilis*, comes from the same verb, *scrutari* (to search or examine) as **scrutiny**. You probably guessed as much. But the root word of that verb is *scruta*—"trash"!

insecticide

This word starts out easy, with **insect**; the ending *–icide* comes from Latin, meaning "killing," as we find in such words as **geno- cide**, **homicide**, **herbicide**, and **pesticide**.

inselar	**insular***
inselarity	**insularity***
inselate	**insulate**
inselation	**insulation**
insentive	**incentive**
insident	**incident**

Correct spelling	*Incorrect spelling*

insidental	**incidental**

insidious

This word came from a Latin word meaning "ambush."

insight/incite (see entry for **incite/insight**)

insinuate, insinuation

This word slips subtly into English from Latin, from *insinuatus*, the past participle of a verb that contains the root word *sinus*, which could mean "curve" or "fold" or "pocket" or "hiding place."

insipid

You recognize the *in-* prefix meaning "not" or "un-," but the delicious origin of this word is the Latin *sapidus,* which has the same meaning as the English word that derived from it—**savory.**

insist, insistent, insistence

insolance	**insolence**
insolant	**insolent**
insolate	**insulate**
insolation	**insulation**

insolence

insolent

insomnia

instill

insular, insularity

The root of these words is the Latin word for "island," *insula.*

insulate

insulation

insulence	**insolence**
insulent	**insolent**

insulin

insurance, insure

intamacy	**intimacy***
intamate	**intimate***

integer

Correct spelling	*Incorrect spelling*

integral

integrity

intelegence	**intelligence***
intelegent	**intelligent***

intellectual, intellectualize

intelligence, intelligent

    The root of these words is a Latin verb that meant "to perceive," formed from two words meaning "to choose among."

interactive, interactivity

intercede

    There are only seven verbs in English that end in –*cede*. In addition to **intercede**, we have **antecede, cede, concede, precede, recede,** and **secede**.

intercollegiate

interest, interested, interesting

    These words have an interesting origin. In Middle English *interest* had the meaning of "legal claim." The word came, by way of Old French, from a Latin verb form meaning "it is of importance." That verb combined the words *inter* (between or among) and *esse* (to be). So, something that was there among people (what brought them together or was keeping them apart?) was important, was of **interest** to them.

interfere, interference, interfering

interogate	**interrogate**
interogation	**interrogation**
interogative	**interrogative**
interogatory	**interrogatory**

interpolate, interpolation

interrogate, interrogation, interrogative, interrogatory

interstate/intrastate

    These words are often pronounced similarly enough so as to cause spelling confusion. It's *interstate* if you're referring to something that happens between or among states. It's *intrastate*

Correct spelling	*Incorrect spelling*

if you mean that it happens within a single state.

interveiw	**interview**
interveneous, intervenious, intervenous	**intravenous***

interview

intimacy, intimate

If you get to know these words well, you'll appreciate that within them lies a Latin adjective, *intimus*, meaning "innermost."

intracate	**intricate***
intraspect	**introspect**

intrastate/interstate (see entry for **interstate/intrastate**)

intravenous, intravenously

The first part of these words is easy: *intra* is Latin for "within." The second part is often misspelled. A friend who is afraid of hypodermics suggests the mnemonic "**v**icious **e**vil **n**eedle **o**perating **u**nder **s**kin." Weird, maybe, but she never misspells this word.

intravert	**introvert**

intrepid

intrest	**interest***
intrested	**interested***
intresting	**interesting***

intricate

This word is peculiar, because it's used only as an adjective, while its exact antonym, **extricate,** is used only as a verb. Both **intricate** and **extricate** come from a Latin root meaning "hindrances" or "perplexities." What makes this little story more intriguing is that the source of **intricate**, *intricare*, evolved through Italian and French to emerge in English as **intrigue**.

intrigue

intrinsic

introspect, introspection, introspective

introvert

inuendo	**innuendo**

Correct spelling   *Incorrect spelling*

Correct spelling	Incorrect spelling

inuendos — **innuendoes**

inumerable — **innumerable**

inundate
> This fancy word for "swamp" or "overwhelm" comes from a Latin verb based on *unda*, meaning "a wave," a root that came into English in **undulate**.

investor

inveterate

invilable — **inviolable**

invincible
> Strip away the negative prefix *in-* and you find a Latin adjective, *vincibilis*, which comes from the verb *vincere*, "to conquer." That verb came into English through Old French to become **vanquish** and more directly in such compounds as **convince** and **evince** and the present participle gave us the name **Vincent**, "conquering."

inviolable

invoice

iodine, iodized

iracable, iraceble, iracible — **irascible***

iradiate — **irradiate**

iradiation — **irradiation**

irascible
> This adjective comes from Latin, *irascibilis*, an adjective formed from the noun *ira*, meaning "anger," which also gave us **ire** and **irate**.

iratate — **irritate**

irate

ireconcilable, ireconcileable, ireconciliable — **irreconcilable**

iregardless — **irregardless***
> Don't worry about spelling this word: it's wrong to use it at all. The correct word is **regardless**.

iresistable, iresistible — **irresistible**

ireverence — **irreverence**

Correct spelling	Incorrect spelling

ireverent	**irreverent**

iridescence, iridescent

iritate	**irritate**

irk

ironic, irony

There's nothing ironic about how these words came into English: the Latin *ironia* came from a Greek word meaning "feigned ignorance."

irracible, irrascible, irrasible	**irascible***

irradiate, irradiation

irrate	**irate**

irreconcilable

This word is difficult to spell because so many people pronounce the final two syllables incorrectly. Just remember that there are only two *i*'s in this word that we use when people don't see eye to eye. (Groan!)

irregardless

This word is wrong. The correct word is **regardless**.

irresistible

irreverence, irreverent

irridescence	**iridescence**
irridescent	**iridescent**

irritate

isalate	**isolate**
isalation	**isolation**
isatope	**isotope**
isel	**isle**
iselate	**isolate**
iselation	**isolation**
isicle	**icicle**

island

An **island** ... *is land!*

Correct spelling	*Incorrect spelling*

isle/aisle (see entry for **aisle/isle**)

isolate

isolation

isotope

isthmus

isulate	**isolate**
isulation	**isolation**

iteration, iterative

These words have developed from the past participle, *iteratum*, of a Latin verb meaning "to repeat."

itinerary

its/it's

Its is a possessive adjective, so it works like the other possessive adjectives, **his**, **her**, **our**, **your**, and **their**—no apostrophe. **It's** with an apostrophe is a contraction (it is), formed just like the contractions **he's** (he is) and **she's** (she is).

itteration	**iteration**
itterative	**iterative**

Correct spelling	*Incorrect spelling*

janitor

January

jealous, jealousy

   This word came into Middle English through Old French, but the
   root meaning shifted—the Latin and Greek root word, *zelos*,
   meant "zeal." That's why we have both **jealous** and **zealous**, from
   a single root.

jelatin	**gelatin**
jelosy	**jealousy***
jelous	**jealous***
jenerik	**generic***
jenial	**genial**
jenoside	**genocide***

jeopardize, jeopardy

jerisdiction	**jurisdiction**
jerisprudence	**jurisprudence**

jewelry

   Variant pronunciations make this word harder to spell. But it's
   simple if you remember that it begins with **jewel**.

jigolo	**gigolo**
joavial	**jovial***
joaviality	**joviality***

jocular, jocularity

jovial, joviality

   These words came through French from Italian, from a word that

---

Correct spelling   *Incorrect spelling*

meant "born under the sign of Jupiter." By Jove!

juckstapose   **juxtapose***

judgment or **judgement, judgmental**
> You can leave the e of **judge** in **judgement**, but not in **judg-mental**. Go figure—it's English!

judicial, judiciary

judicious

judishial   **judicial**

judishiary   **judiciary**

judishious   **judicious**

juggle

jugular

jurisdiction

jurisprudence

justify, justifiable, justification

juvenile

juxtapose, juxtaposition
> These words come from French, composed of two words of Latin origin—*juxta*, meaning "near," and *poser*, "to place." By the way, that *juxta* evolved in Old French and Middle English into **joust**, the sport of fighting close together.

Correct spelling   *Incorrect spelling*

Incorrect spelling	Correct spelling
kadaver	**cadaver**
kafeen	**caffeine**

kaffeeklatsch

> This was the original form of what's now generally spelled **coffee klatch** or **coffee klatsch.** It's a German word formed from the words for "coffee" and "chat."

| *kalamine* | **calamine** |

kaleidoscope

> This word was formed from three Greek words, somewhat modified: *kalos* (beautiful), *eidos* (form), and *skopein* (to see).

kalossal	**colossal**
kamaflage	**camouflage***
kamaraderie	**camaraderie**

kamikaze

> This word is Japanese for "wind of gods."

kangaroo

kantalope	**cantaloupe***
kantankerous	**cantankerous**
kanumdrum	**conumdrum**
kapacious	**capacious**

karaoke

> This word comes from Japanese: "kara" comes from *karappo*, meaning empty, and *oke* is the abbreviation of *okesutura*, from the English **orchestra.**

karat/carat/caret/carrot (see entry for **carat/caret/ carrot/karat**)

Correct spelling   *Incorrect spelling*

kareoke, karioke	**karaoke***
karisma	**charisma**
karkas	**carcass**

karma

> This word is a rare borrowing from Sanskrit, from a word meaning "deed."

karrisma	**charisma**
karsinoma	**carcinoma**
katastrophy	**catastrophe**
katharsis	**catharsis**
keibasa	**kielbasa***
kenetic	**kinetic**

Keogh

> The retirement plan is named after Eugene J. Keogh. Will knowing that fact help you spell the word correctly? Maybe.

kerasene	**kerosene***

kerchief

kereoke, kerioke	**karaoke***
keresene	**kerosene***

kernel/colonel (see entry for **colonel/kernel**)

kerosene

> This word was coined as a trademark in 1854 from the Greek *keros* (wax). **Kerosine** is an accepted variant spelling.

keyosk	**kiosk***

khaki, khakis

> This word is Hindi, meaning "dusty"—appropriate for the dust-colored fabric popular in India and Pakistan.

kibitz

> This term for looking on and offering unwanted advice comes from Yiddish, originally from German.

kibosh

> When you put the kibosh an a plan or an idea, you're using a word of uncertain origin. But at least you know how to spell the word.

Correct spelling	*Incorrect spelling*

kielbasa
> This word is Polish for "sausage."

kilo, kilobyte, kilogram, kilohertz, kilometer

kindergarten
> This word is German, combining the words for "children" and "garden" to designate a place where kids grow together.

kinesiology

kinesthetic

kinetic

kinnesiology	**kinesiology**
kinnesthetic	**kinesthetic**
kinnetic	**kinetic**

kiosk
> Although this word came into English from French, where it's *kiosque*, we end it in –*k*, which is closer to the Turkish and Persian roots, *koshk* and *kushk*.

kismet
> This word for "fate" or "good fortune" comes from a Turkish word meaning "portion, something allotted."

kitsch
> This word is from a German verb meaning "to put together sloppily."

klamidia	**chlamydia**

klatch or **klatsch**
> This word, as in **coffee klatch** or **coffee klatsch** (originally spelled **kaffeeklatsch**), is German, *klatsch*, meaning "chat."

klorine	**chlorine**

knell
> This word, now used only in such expressions as "death **knell**," is a noun or a verb for signaling disaster or destruction.

knight/night
> **Knight** was once a military rank but is now an honorific title.
> **Night** is the opposite of day.

Correct spelling	*Incorrect spelling*

knit/nit

To **knit** is to work with yarn, to furrow the brow, or for muscles or bones to heal. A **nit** is the egg or young of a parasitic insect.

knitpicking   **nitpicking***

knot/not

A **knot** is strings tied or tangled, a difficult problem, a hard place in a tree or in muscles, and a measure of speed (one nautical mile or about 1.15 statute miles per hour). **Not** is a negative.

knowledge, knowledgeable, knowledgeably

kohlrabi

kolesterol	**cholesterol**
kollateral	**collateral**
komplasent	**complacent**
korogated	**corrugated**
kroshay	**crochet**
kurt	**curt**

With a capital *K*, this is a name. But if you mean "rudely brief and abrupt," it's **curt**, from the same Latin root, *curtus*, that evolved into **curtail**.

kwizine   **cuisine***

Correct spelling   *Incorrect spelling*

| Correct spelling | Incorrect spelling |

labarinth, laberinth — **labyrinth**

laboratory
    The usual pronunciation of this word drops the first *o*, which tends to obscure the core, **labor**.

labyrinth, labyrinthine

lacadaisical — **lackadaisical**

lacconic, lacconnic — **laconic***

lacivious — **lascivious**

lackadaisical

laconic
    This great word to describe someone who uses few words comes from an alternative name for the Spartans of ancient Greece, who were famous for being tough and short on words.

lacuna

laff — **laugh**

lagniappe
    This word for a small gift that a store owner gives a customer with a purchase came into English from Louisiana French. It came from the Spanish, who got it from a word in Quechua (the language spoken by a South American Indian tribe) that meant "to give more." That explanation may not help you spell this word, but at least you have an impressive way to refer to an extra or unexpected gift or benefit.

laid

lair

lakonic — **laconic**

languid

Incorrect spelling	Correct spelling

lanyap — **lagniappe***

larangitis — **laryngitis**

laranx — **larynx**

larceny

largess or **largesse**

This word came into Middle English from Old French, where *large* meant "generous," a development from Latin, *largus*, "abundant."

laringitis — **laryngitis**

larinx — **larynx**

larjess — **largess**

larnix, larnyx — **larynx**

larseny, larsony — **larceny**

laryngitis, larynx

lascivious

latitude

latte

This very recent addition to English is a shortened form of **caffe latte**, an Italian term, originally *caffè e latte* (coffee and milk), for espresso mixed with hot or steamed milk.

lattitude — **latitude**

laugh, laughable, laughter

lavatory

laxative

lay

lead/led

Lead is a metal or the graphite/clay mixture used in pencils. **Led** is the past participle of the verb **lead** ("we lead now, we led yesterday").

leagal — **legal**

leagality — **legality**

Correct spelling   *Incorrect spelling*

leagalize	**legalize**

league

Sometimes two words happen to develop into the same spelling; that's the case here. **League** meaning "association" came from a Latin verb meaning "to bind," which evolved through Italian, Old French, and Middle English. **League** meaning "unit of distance" had Celtic roots; the word and meaning passed into medieval Latin and then Middle English. That's why **league** and **league** have nothing in common but their spelling.

leak/leek

Leak is an escape or loss, the means through which something escapes or is lost, or the action. **Leek** is a plant related to the onion. To remember the spelling of the first of these homophones, think of the vowels in "s*ea*l a l*ea*k."

leanience	**lenience***
leaniency	**leniency***
leanient	**lenient***
leathal	**lethal**
leaway	**leeway**

led/lead (see entry for **lead/led**)

leek/leak (see entry for **leak/leek**)

leenience	**lenience***
leeniency	**leniency***
leenient	**lenient***

leeway

legable	**legible**

legacy

legal, legality, legalize

legible, legibility

legislate, legislation, legislator, legislature

legitimate

Correct spelling	*Incorrect spelling*

legue   **league**

leisure

One of six exceptions to the "*i* before *e* except after *c*" rule. The others are **either, neither, seize** and **seizure,** and **weird.** This word started out in Latin from the verb, *licere,* meaning "to be permitted," which is the root of **license.** But then it evolved through Old French and Middle English into its current meaning and spelling. Remember the first syllable by thinking of the **lei** you'll get when you arrive in Hawaii to begin your life of **leisure.**

lenience, leniency, lenient

These words came from the present participle, *leniens,* of a Latin verb meaning "to pacify," from an adjective meaning "soft."

lens, lenses

The unusual spelling of the singular of this noun is because the word was borrowed directly from Latin. Also unusual is the meaning of the borrowed word, "lentil"—because the double con- vex shape of the first **lens** resembled a lentil.

lethal

lethargic, lethargy

leukemia

leutenant, leutenent   **lieutenant***

levee/levy

A **levee** is raised land that contains a river or irrigated field. It's borrowed from French, the past participle of the verb *lever,* "to raise." **Levy** is a verb or a noun for imposing or collecting a tax, drafting into military service, or confiscating property—all ways of raising what the government needs. This word is also from the same Old French source, but it evolved through Middle English.

leverage

levitate, levity

levrage   **leverage**

levy/levee (see entry for **levee/levy**)

lexical, lexicon

Correct spelling   *Incorrect spelling*

liability

liable/libel

> **Liable** indicates a legal obligation or a likelihood. **Libel** is written or graphic defamation.

liaison

> This word, French for relationship or tie, is easier to spell if you think of the —a— as being **and** to link two i's.

liar

liason	**liaison**
libarian	**librarian**
libary	**library**
libbidinous	**libidinous**
libbido	**libido**

libel/liable (see entry for **liable/libel**)

liberty, libertarian

libido, libidinous

library, librarian

liccorice	**licorice**

license

> This word evolved through Old French and Middle English from the Latin noun, *licentia*, from a verb that meant "to be permitted." That's why we have the differing meanings of "natural freedom" and "legal permission."

licentious

licit

licor	**liquor**

licorice

lier	**liar**
liesure	**leisure***

lieutenant

> This word is French, from two words that mean "place holder."
> We have the first of those words in the expression **in lieu of** and

---

Correct spelling	*Incorrect spelling*

the second in **tenant**. (The spelling of this word is more complicated for the British, because they pronounce the *u* in this word as an *f*.)

light

lightening/lightning

> **Lightening** is a form of the verb **lighten**. **Lightning** is atmospheric electricity.

lightning/lightening (see entry for **lightening/lightning**)

Incorrect spelling	Correct spelling
ligitamate, ligitimate	**legitimate**
likrish	**licorice**
likwidate	**liquidate**
likwify	**liquefy***
lim	**limb**

This word is easy to spell if you think of a **limb** as being **limber**. (The words seem to come from different origins, so the similarity is probably just a nice coincidence.)

Incorrect spelling	Correct spelling
limazine	**limousine***

limb

Incorrect spelling	Correct spelling
limmasine	**limousine***
limmit, limmitation	**limit, limitation**

limousine

> This vehicle got its name from *Limousin*, a region in France. The French pronounce that troublesome syllable –*ou*- as *ooo*— the sound that many people make when a **limousine** passes. But you can also think of those two letters as standing for what most people think about the lucky passenger: "**O**h, yo**u** ...."

lineal, linear

lingerie

Incorrect spelling	Correct spelling
linneal	**lineal**
linnear	**linear**

linoleum

liposuction

Correct spelling	Incorrect spelling

liquedate	**liquidate**

liquefy

> Only four verbs end in –*efy*: **liquefy**, **putrefy**, **rarefy**, and **stupefy**. (A second spelling, **liquify**, is also acceptable.)

liquid

liquidate

liquidity

liquify	**liquefy***

liquor

liscence, liscense, lisence, lisense	**license***

litany

lite	**light**

> Don't be misled by all the food products promoting with this popular misspelling. It may be popular, but it's still a misspelling—so far.

liter/litter

> **Liter** is correct for a metric unit of measurement. If you mean to leave trash where it doesn't belong, that's **litter**.

literacy

literal, literally

literasy	**literacy**

literate

literati

literature

literer	**litterer**
litering	**littering**

litigant, litigation, litigious

> These words come from Latin, but that won't help you spell them correctly. What about if you think of the beginning letters as standing for "*l*egal *i*mpressive *t*erminology *i*n *g*obbledygook"?

litiny	**litany**

litmus

> When you talk about a "**litmus** test," you should thank the lichen

Correct spelling	*Incorrect spelling*

that provided scientists with the pigment that indicates acidity and alkalinity. The word **litmus** goes back to a Middle English word of Scandinavian origin, meaning roughly "color moss," since the plant was early used to produce dye.

littany	**litany**
litter/liter (see entry for **liter/litter**)	
litterer, littering	
litteracy	**literacy**
litteral, litterally	**literal, literally**
litterasy	**literacy**
litterate	**literate**
litterati, litteratti	**literati**
litterature	**literature**
littigant	**litigant***
littigation	**litigation***
littigious	**litigious***
littiny	**litany**
littmus	**litmus***

lo/low

    Lo is an interjection from Middle English, now used almost exclusively in such expressions as "**lo** and behold" "**lo** these many years." It's also a shortened form of **low** that should be used only when space requires it. **Low** is the opposite of high.

loan/lone

    Loan is something that is lent or (informally) the act of lending. **Lone** means "sole" or "isolated." It's a Middle English shortening of **alone**. Just remember that the heart of **lone** is **one**.

loath, loathe, loathing

    These words confuse some people. **Loath** is an adjective: you are **loath** to do something. **Loathe** is a verb: you **loathe** doing something.

locamotive	**locomotive**

Correct spelling	*Incorrect spelling*

locconic, locconnic	**laconic***

loco

locomotive

lone/loan (see entry for **loan/lone**)

loneliness, lonely

longevity

loose/lose
> These two words are almost homophones—close enough to mislead some people into confusing them. **Loose** is the opposite of tight and is rarely used as a verb; we usually use **loosen**. (There's also the adverb, **loosely**, not tightly.) **Lose** is always a verb, with the related forms **losing** and **loser**.

loquacious, loquacity

lose/loose (see entry for **loose/lose**)

lovable (or **loveable**)

loveliness, lovely

low/lo (see entry for **lo/low**)

loyal, loyalty

luau

lubricant, lubricate, lubrication

lucid, lucidity

lucius	**luscious**

lucrative
> This word comes from the same Latin source as **lucre**, a word that once meant "profit" but now is used only in the expression "filthy **lucre**."

ludicrous

lugubrious

lugzuriant	**luxuriant**
lugzuriate	**luxuriate**
lugzurious	**luxurious**

Correct spelling	*Incorrect spelling*

Incorrect spelling	Correct spelling
lugzury	**luxury**
lukemia	**leukemia**

luminescent, luminescence, luminous
>   The Latin root used in combination with endings was *lumin-* (light).

lurid

luscious

lutenant	**lieutenant***

luxuriant, luxuriate

luxurious, luxury

luxurriant	**luxuriant**
luxurriate	**luxuriate**
luxurrious	**luxurious**
luxurry	**luxury**
lyer	**liar**

lying

macaroni

macaroon

maccaroni   **macaroni**

maccaroon   **macaroon**

Machiavellian

This adjective pays tribute to Niccolò Machiavelli, a 16th-century
Italian who advocated using any means to achieve political ends.

machine

mackerel

macro

macrobiotic

magnanimity, magnanimous

We got these words for "nobility of character" directly from Latin,
magnanimus, an adjective that combined *magnus* (great) and *animus*
(mind or spirit). Being **magnanimous** is beyond just **equanimity**
(even-tempered) and far from **pusillanimity** (cowardly).

maintenance

makrel   **mackerel**

malevolence, malevolent

These words derive from Latin, *male volens*, "wishing evil."
They're antonyms of **benevolence** and **benevolent.**

malfeasance

This word is to a public official what **malpractice** is to a professional. The second part of this noun comes from an Old French
word derived from a Latin word based on the verb meaning "to
do." So the verb core of this word is related to **feat** and **defeat**.

| Correct spelling | *Incorrect spelling* |

malice, malicious

malign, malignant

These words come from a Middle English verb meaning "to attack," that came through Old French from a Latin adjective, *malignus*.

maliscious, malishus **malicious**

mall/maul

A **mall** is a shopping center, but it was originally a shady public walkway, named after The Mall in London, whose name derived from the fact that a game called pall-mall ("mallet ball") was played there. **Maul** is a noun for a type of hammer used in splitting wood and a verb for splitting wood or, more generally, handling roughly.

mammogram

manacure **manicure**

manafesto **manifesto**

manager, managerial

mañana

This word that we use to mean "later," indefinitely, is Spanish for "tomorrow."

manecure **manicure**

manetenance **maintenance**

maneuver

This word came into English through French from two Latin words meaning "to work by hand." (There's a variant, chiefly used in British English, that's closer to the French spelling.) It may help to remember that the –eu- combination is used in a lot of words that came from French, such as **amateur, milieu, chauffeur, connoisseur, entrepreneur,** and **grandeur.**

manicure

manifesto

mannacure **manicure**

mannafesto **manifesto**

mannicure **manicure**

| **Correct spelling** | *Incorrect spelling* |

mannifesto	**manifesto**

mano a mano
> This term for close combat is sometimes used to mean "one on one" (probably from confusion over the meaning of *mano*), but it's actually Spanish for "hand to hand."

manual

manuever	**maneuver***

manufacture

manule	**manual**
manuver	**maneuver***

maraschino
> We borrowed this word from the Italians, although we usually don't pronounce it as they do. The root is *marasca*, "bitter wild cherry."

marble

mariage, marij	**marriage**

marijuana
> There's also an older spelling, **marihuana,** which is how the word was spelled in Mexican Spanish.

marital
> This adjective has a single *r*, not the double *rr* of **marriage** and **marry**, because it comes from the French word for "marry," *marier*.

marriage

marrital	**marital***

marshal/martial
> The first of these words is a term used for certain officers or the act of enlisting and arranging forces or resources. The second word refers to fighting, from Mars, the god of war. It's also used in the term **court-martial**, a military legal process.

martial/marshal (see entry for **marshal/martial**)

martyr, martyrdom

masochism, masochist

Correct spelling	*Incorrect spelling*

mastectomy

mathematical, mathematics

mattress

maul/mall (see entry for **mall/maul**)

mauve

   This name for a color in the area of purple, violet, and lilac comes from the French, who got the word *malva* from the Romans, meaning "mallow," a plant related to the marsh mallow that becomes candy. Our word **mallow** came into Middle English from the same Old French word that became the color **mauve**.

maverick

   This word for any member of a group who refuses to wear a label or adhere to group beliefs or rules is only about 150 years old. In 1840 a rancher in Texas, Samuel Maverick, neglected to brand his cattle, so the term **maverick** eventually was applied to any unbranded cattle and then the term spread to people.

maximum

maybe

mayonnaise

measly

   This word is easier to spell if you know that it's related to **measles**. The original meaning was "infected with measles."

mecanic	**mechanic**
mecanical	**mechanical**
mecanism	**mechanism**

mechanic, mechanical

mechanism

medal/meddle/mettle

   Medal is short for **medallion**. (Although it may resemble the word **metal**, it actually comes from an Old Italian word for a coin worth half a denarius, from a Latin word meaning "middle"— because the coin had a value midway between nothing and a denarius. Logical!) **Meddle** is to interfere, from a Middle English

Correct spelling	*Incorrect spelling*

word meaning "to mix." **Mettle** refers to character, temperament, courage, spirit—a word rarely used anymore except in the expression "to test someone's **mettle**."

medallion

meddle/medal/mettle (see entry for **medal/meddle/ mettle**)

Incorrect spelling	Correct spelling
medeate	**mediate**
medeation	**mediation**
medeator	**mediator**
medeival, medeval	**medieval**

mediate, mediation, mediator

medical, medicinal, medicine

medieval

medley

meesly	**measly***

mega

This word that is gaining in popularity comes from a Greek word meaning "great." As a scientific prefix, it means one million, a very great number.

megalomania

melancholy

melanoma

melee or mêlée

This word for a confused fight or struggle is French, meaning "mixed." It developed in Old French from the same Latin root that developed in Middle English, again with the help of Old French, into **meddle** and **medley**.

memento

memo, memos

memorabilia, memorable

memorandum

memorial

memoriam

This word is used in the expression "in memoriam," a Latin phrase meaning "into memory."

memory, memorize

menace

mentor

This word now in trendy use in business was the name of a friend whom Odysseus trusted to serve as a guide for his son Telemachus. But Mentor got credit then and down through the ages for good work that was actually done by Athena in disguise.

mercenary

mere

meringue

The *–ngue* ending occurs only in **meringue, harangue,** and **tongue**—all words from the French.

mesa

This word for a flat-topped hill is Spanish for "table."

mesly   **measly***

mesmerize

metabolic, metabolism

metal, metallic

metamorphosis

metaphor, metaphorical

It's easier to spell metaphor if you know that it comes from a Latin word, *metaphora*, derived from a Greek verb that meant "to trans-fer." You recognize *meta* (change), such as in **metamorphosis,** but you may not recognize *phora*, such as we find in **amphora.**

meteorology

meticulous

We use this word in generally positive ways now, but the Latin root, *meticulosus*, meant timid and the root, *metus*, meant "fear."

mettal, mettallic   **metal, metallic**

Correct spelling   *Incorrect spelling*

mettle/medal/meddle (see entry for **medal/meddle/ mettle**)

mezly   **measly***

mezmerize   **mesmerize**

midwife

might/mite

  The first of these homophones is used as a verb and a noun
  meaning "strength." The second is a tiny arachnid, a small object,
  or something of little value.

milatant   **militant**

milenium, milennium   **millennium***

milieu

  This word is pure French, as you might guess from the *eu* such as
  we find in **amateur** and **maneuver**, to mention only two more
  examples. We use this word as synonymous with "environment"
  or "surroundings," but the original meaning in French was "center" or "middle": *mi-* (middle) and *lieu* (place), the second word
  also making it into English in **lieutenant** ("place holder") and in
  the expression **in lieu of**.

milionaire   **millionaire**

milisia   **militia**

militant

military

militent   **militant**

militia

millatant   **militant**

millennium

  This is one of the 10 most commonly used words at this point in
  our calendar—and one of the most commonly misspelled. It's
  straight Latin, from *milla* (thousand, as in **millipede**) and *annum*
  (year, as in **per annum** and **annual**). Just remember, there are
  two *l*'s and two *n*'s in **millennium**.

Correct spelling   *Incorrect spelling*

millieu	**milieu***
millionaire	
millisia	**militia**
millitant	**militant**
millitary	**military**
millitent	**militant**

mimic, mimicked, mimicking, mimicry
  These words come from a Latin form, *mimicus*, of a Greek word
  that derived from *momos*, "imitator." That root we recognize as
  the origin of **mime** and a word that was coined as a trademark,
  mimeograph.

mimosa
  This name for a genus of tropical plants, shrubs, and trees has
  entered into use recently for a drink made of champagne and
  (usually) orange juice.

minamum	**minimum**
minarel	**mineral***
minature	**miniature**

miner/minor
  The first of these people works in a **mine** and the second is
  someone not yet of legal age.

mineral
  If you dig a little into this word, you'll find **mine**.

miniature

minimum

miniscule
  Poor spellers, rejoice! This spelling has recently been accepted as
  a variant of **minuscule**.

miniture	**miniature**
minneral	**mineral***
minniture	**miniature**

minor/miner (see entry for **miner/minor**)

Correct spelling	*Incorrect spelling*

minuscule

This word came from a Latin adjective, *minusculus*, "very small," a diminutive of *minor*, "smaller." It was used throughout the Middle Ages and beyond to refer to small letters, as opposed to *majuscule*, capital letters.

minutia, minutiae

These words (singular and plural) come straight from Latin, where *minutia* meant "smallness."

miopia	**myopia***
miopic	**myopic***
miral	**mural**
miriad	**myriad***

mirror

misaginist	**misogynist***
misaginy	**misogyny***

mischief, mischievous

The word **mischief** came into Middle English from Old French, where the earlier form meant "misfortune," with its roots in the Latin word for "head" that developed into such words as **chief**, **chef**, **kerchief**, **achieve**, and **captain**.

misconstrue

misile	**missile***

mislead

This means "to lead astray, in the present tense. The spelling of the past tense confuses some people: it's **misled**, since the past tense of **lead** is **led**.

misnomer

misogynist, misogyny

These words derived from a Greek word that combined the word for "hate," which we also find in **misanthropy** and **misogamy**, and the word for "women," which we also find in **gynecology**.

missal/missile

A **missal** is a prayer book used in the Catholic mass, named after

Correct spelling	*Incorrect spelling*

the final Latin words "*ite, missa est*" ("Go, it is sent"). A **missile** is an object that is projected (sent) as a weapon, a projectile.

missconstrue	**misconstrue**

missile/missal (see entry for **missal/missile**)

missiletoe	**mistletoe**
misslead	**mislead***
missnomer	**misnomer**

misspell, misspelled, misspelling
This word and related forms may look odd, but the formation is logical: the prefix *mis-* and **spell**.

misstate
The spelling of **misstate** may look odd, but it's logical: the prefix *mis-* and **state**.

missunderstand	**misunderstand**
misterious	**mysterious**
mistery	**mystery**

mistletoe

misunderstand

mit	**mitt**
mitagate	**mitigate**

mite/might (see entry for **might/mite**)

miten	**mitten**

mitigate

miton	**mitten**

mitt

mitten

mittigate	**mitigate**

mnemonic
Since we don't pronounce the beginning *m-*, we sometimes forget it's there. Since this word means a device used to help remember, it seems only appropriate to offer a **mnemonic** here: think of the first two letters as standing for "*m*emory *n*udge."

Correct spelling	*Incorrect spelling*

mocasin, mocassin, moccassin	**moccasin**

mocha

model, modeling

modus operandi

This term, which we usually abbreviate as M.O., is pure Latin for "means of operating."

moka	**mocha**

molasses

This word is a rare (and disguised) borrowing from Portuguese, *melaço*, from a Latin word that derived from *mel*, "honey."

mollify

momento	**memento**

This is an object that reminds us of something; it begins with *mem-* just as we find in **memory** and **remember**.

monalith	**monolith**
monalithic	**monolithic**
monnopolistic	**monopolistic**
monnopoly	**monopoly**

monogamous, monogamy

monolith, monolithic

mononucleosis

monopolistic, monopoly

moot/mute

These words are not true homophones, but they're pronounced enough alike to confuse people. **Moot** means arguable or of no significance, as in "a moot point." **Mute** means silent.

moral/morale

These related words, although not really homophones, confuse people sometimes. **Moral** as an adjective is synonymous with ethical and as a noun means "lesson." **Morale** is an emotional state, so just think of the final —e as standing for emotion.

morale/moral (see entry for **moral/morale**)

morbid, morbidity

Correct spelling	*Incorrect spelling*

morf   **morph**

This recent coinage comes from **metamorphose**; the root
—*morph*- is from the Greek word for "form."

morgage   **mortgage***

moribund

morose

morph

mortafied   **mortified**

mortgage

This word came into Middle English from Old French, composed
of the word *mort*, "dead" or "death," of Latin origin, and *gage*,
"pledge," of Germanic origin. When somebody wanted to borrow
money against property that he or she would inherit when a par-
ent died, the property used a collateral would be a "dead pledge"
or a "death pledge."

mortician

mortified, mortify

mortuary

mosquito, mosquitoes (or **mosquitos**)

This is a Spanish word, meaning "little fly."

motley

moxie

This word was popular more than a few decades ago to label
someone with sprit, energy, and/or courage. It's a word that goes
back only as far as the trademark name for a soft drink, Moxie.

mozzarella

mulch

mural

murder, murderous

murmur, murmuring

murral   **mural**

| **Correct spelling** | *Incorrect spelling* |

mustard/mustered

The first of these homophones is a condiment. The second is the past tense of the verb "to **muster**."

muster

This word, meaning "to summon or gather" or a gathering (especially of troops), is also used in the expression "To pass **muster**" (to measure up to some standard or expectation).

mustered/mustard (see entry for **mustard/mustered**)

mutate, mutation

mute/moot (see entry for **moot/mute**)

myopia, myopic

This word comes from a Greek word meaning "to close" and "eye." The first root we discover as well in **mystery** and **mystic** and the second we see in **Cyclops** and **optic**.

myriad

This word comes directly from a Greek word meaning, as in English, "countless" or "ten thousand."

mysaginist	**misogynist***
mysaginy	**misogyny***
mysogynist	**misogynist***
mysogyny	**misogyny***

mysterious, mystery

<table>
</table>

nabor   **neighbor***

naïve

This word is from the Latin meaning "to be born." It's **native** without the *–t*, with the implication that the person has never left his or her home town. Its current meaning is innocent, naturally simple, or unsophisticated.

namonia   **pneumonia***

narcissism, narcissistic, narcissus

Narcissus was the Greek god who fell in love with himself when he saw his reflection in a pool of water and rejected others' love. These words mean "conceited," although **narcissus** also is a variety of spring flower.

narrow

nascent

Although this word contains the letters *scent*, it comes from a Latin word meaning "being born," a sense we take figuratively as beginning to exit or develop.

Naugahyde

This is a trademark used for vinyl-coated fabrics. It's not technically a hide—and there's no such animal as a *nauga*.

naught

This word derives from an Old English word that combined the words for "no" and "thing." A variant spelling is **nought**.

naughty

This word comes from the same Old English root as **naught**, a word that combined the words for "no" and "thing."

Correct spelling   *Incorrect spelling*

nausea

This word comes from the Greek for "ship," the vehicle that can cause nausea in the form of seasickness. We find the same root in **nautical**.

nauseam

We use this word in the expression "**ad nauseam**," which is pure Latin for "to the point of nausea."

nauseous

nauseum	**nauseam***
naut	**naught***

nautical

nauty	**naughty***

navigate

nayber	**neighbor***
neace	**niece***

Neanderthal

Neapolitan

This term generally used for a brick of ice cream of two to four layers of different flavors (usually chocolate, vanilla, and strawberry) is a Middle English word based on the Latin *neapolitanus*, the adjective for Naples, which was originally called *Neapolis*.

neccessary	**necessary***
neccessitate	**necessitate**
neccessity	**necessity**

necessary

Only one –c, but a double –ss is essential when spelling this word.

necessitate, necessity

neckerchief

necklace

nectarine

Here's a mnemonic to help you remember how to spell this fruit: "She washed off the *tar* from the **nectarine**."

Correct spelling	*Incorrect spelling*

neece	**niece***
neether	**neither***
nefarious	
nefew	**nephew***
negligence	
negotiate	
neibor	**neighbor***
neice	**niece***

neighbor
This word comes from Old English for "near-by farmer." This word is a famous exception to the "*i* before *e* except after *c*" rule—"except in words like **neighbor** and **weigh**."

neither
One of six exceptions to the *i* before *e* except after *c* rule. The others are **either, leisure, weird,** and **seize** and **seizure**.

nell	**knell***

nemesis
This word is the name of the Greek goddess of retribution.

nemonic	**mnemonic***

neophyte
This word comes from the Greek word for a "new plant" and means an "amateur" or "beginner."

neopolitan	**Neapolitan***
nepharious	**nefarious**

nephew
This word is French. The Latin root is *nepos*, which gives us **nepotism** and is related to *neptia*, which becomes **niece**.

nepotism
We use this word for any favoritism shown to relatives or friends, but the use was originally far more restricted. The root of this word is the Latin word for "nephew," *nepos*.

nerd

Correct spelling	*Incorrect spelling*

nervana   **nirvana**

nerve-racking

There's no need to get distressed over this spelling, since the word can also be spelled **nerve-wracking**.

netiquette

This new word is a combination of the words Inter*net* and *eti-quette*.

neurological, neurology

The root of these words is *neuro-* from the Latin for "nerve" and refers to the state of the nervous system in health and disease.

neuroses, neurosis, neurotic

newmatik   **pneumatic***

newmonia   **pneumonia***

nexus

nialism   **nihilism***

nialistic   **nihilist***

niche

This word comes into English straight from French, where it developed from the Latin verb meaning "to nest."

nickel

Nickel is found in an ore that often fools people looking for copper ore. That's why the German name for nickel ore is *Kupfernickel*, "copper demon."

niece

This word comes from French. The Latin root is *neptia*, which is related to *nepos*, a word that evolves into **nephew** and **nepotism**.

niether   **neither***

nifty

niggardly

This word got its 15 minutes of fame (or infamy) in 1999 when a government worker used it and found that it offended some people because of its similarity to the "N word"—an incident that generated headlines and scores of opinion pieces. Almost lost in

---

Correct spelling   *Incorrect spelling*

the uproar was the fact that there's no relationship at all between the two words. **Niggard** came into Middle English from Scandinavian origins, while the truly offensive word goes back to the Latin word for "black." So, beware if you use this word—and at least spell it correctly.

night/knight (see entry for **knight/night**)

nihilism, nihilist

This philosophy and its adherents presume that social and political order should be reduced to nothing. If structures are reduced to nothing, I alone remain—and it's logical that the only vowel in these words is –i.

nil

nilon	**nylon**
nimf, nimph	**nymph**

nineteen, ninetieth, ninety

ninny

Don't be a ninny. Remember there are three –n's in this word.

ninth

Ninth is one of the few exceptions to the rule that keeps the final –e before suffixes that begin with consonants.

nirvana

nit/knit (see entry for **knit/nit**)

nitch	**niche***
nite	**night**

Although the shorter spelling of this word has become popular, it's still incorrect.

nitpicking

The first **nitpicking** involved plucking the eggs or young (nits) of parasitic insects from the body.

noch	**notch**
nockious	**noxious**

nocturnal

noggahide	**Naugahyde***

Correct spelling	*Incorrect spelling*

nomad

Here's a mnemonic to help you remember how to spell this word: "The **nomad** was *mad* when forced to go *no*where."

nomanate   **nominate**

nom de guerre

This word translates from the French as "war name." Originally French soldiers assumed a name when entering the military.

nom de plume

This word translates from the French as "pen name." It's a pseudonym used by writers who don't want their real names used in print.

nomenclature

A friend offers this mnemonic for **nomenclature**: "There are *no men-* in this word."

nominal

nominate

nonchalance, nonchalant

It might help to know that these French words share the same origin as **chauffeur**, going back to a Latin verb for "to be warm." The Old French root verb meant "to be unconcerned," which we could translate literally and figuratively as "to remain cool."

noncommittal

nonshalance   **nonchalance***
nonshalant   **nonchalant***

nostalgia

This word derives from the Greek word *nostos*, meaning "home," and the suffix *–algia*, meaning "pain," as in **neuralgia**.

nostril

not/knot (see entry for **knot/not**)

nota bene

This Latin expression, "note well," we usually abbreviate as **N.B.**

notafication   **notification**
notafy   **notify**

| **Correct spelling** | *Incorrect spelling* |

notarize, notary

notch

notery	**notary**
noterize	**notarize**

notice, noticeable, noticeably

notify, notification

nought

This is a variant spelling for **naught.**

nouveau riche

This word is French for "newly rich." It's a derogatory term given to individuals who suddenly acquire wealth, but don't conform to the customs of the class they now belong to.

novice

To spell this word correctly, remember that a **novice** has *no vice*—but often makes a lot of mistakes.

noxious

nuance

nuclear

This word is often mispronounced and thus misspelled. This tip might help: **nuclear** is *unclear* with the first two letters reversed.

nucleus

nucular	**nuclear***

nugget

nuisance

This word is from the Latin meaning "to kill or harm." The meaning has weakened over the years, as we now apply the word to anything or anyone troubling, annoying, or just inconvenient.

nuke

nulify	**nullify***

null

This word, which as a modifier means "having no legal force," "invalid," "insignificant," or "amounting to nothing" and as a noun

Correct spelling	*Incorrect spelling*

means "zero," comes through French from a Latin word, *nullus*, which also gave us **nullify**.

nullify

Use a –*ll*- when spelling this word or you to make nothing out of something. This word is from Latin, meaning "to make nothing."

numb

numeric, numerical

numonic	**mnemonic***
nurd	**nerd**
nurture	
nurvana	**nirvana**
nusance	**nuisance***
nylon	
nymph	

oagel	**ogle**
oager	**ogre***
oanerous	**onerous***
oarnge	**orange***

oasis, oases

    The Greeks imported this word, which meant "a dwelling place," from Egypt. Since the singular ends in *–is*, the plural is formed with *–es,* as in **analysis—analyses, crisis—crises, hypothesis—hypotheses, parenthesis—parentheses,** and **thesis—theses**.

obay	**obey**

obedience, obedient

    The word *die* is found in the middle of **obedience** and **obedient**. Here's a mnemonic to help you remember: "The naughty boy would sooner *die* than be **obedient**."

obey

obfuscate

    This word comes straight from the Latin, *obfuscare,* for "to darken" and means "to obscure, stupefy, or confuse."

obleek	**oblique**

obligate, obligation, oblige

oblique

oblivion, oblivious

obnoxious

obsequious

    This word has shifted slightly in meaning over the centuries, from its root in Latin, meaning "compliant."

Correct spelling   *Incorrect spelling*

observance, observant, observe

It's easier to spell these words if you know that they come from the same Latin root, *servare* (to watch), as **serve** and **servant**.

obstacle

This word from Latin means to "stand against."

obstanate	**obstinate***
obstensible	**ostensible**
obstentatious	**ostentatious**

obstetrician

This word comes from the Latin *obstetrix* ("midwife"). Now it means a doctor who specializes in **obstetrics** and childbirth.

obsticle	**obstacle***

obstinate

Remember how to spell this word with this mnemonic: "The **obstinate** goat looked at the *tin* can and then *ate* it."

obstreperous

This word is from the Latin meaning to "to clamor against" or "to make a lot of noise before others." A suggested mnemonic: "A case of *strep* throat kept the **obstreperous** child quiet."

obstucle	**obstacle***

obtuse

If you end this blunt word with *–use*, you can *use* it correctly.

obvious

obzervance	**observance***
obzervant	**observant***
obzerve	**observe***

occasion, occasional, occasionally

These words have a double *–cc* and a single *–s*. It might help to remember that there are also a double *–cc* and a single *–s* in the word **accidents**—which happen on **occasion**.

occean, occeanic	**ocean, oceanic***
occillate	**oscillate**

Correct spelling	*Incorrect spelling*

occur, occurred, occurrence, occurring
Double the last consonant before adding the suffixes *–ed, –ence,* and *–ing* because the accent is on the last syllable of the base word **occur**.

ocean, oceanic
The Greeks thought that the world was a flat disk and that a river encircled it. They gave the name "Ocean" to the river they believed surrounded the world.

ocillate   **oscillate**

o'clock
The apostrophe indicates that this word is a contraction; it was once "of the clock."

octopus

ocur   **occur***

ocurred   **occurred***

ocurrence   **occurrence***

ocurring   **occurring***

oddisy   **odyssey***

oddity

odisy   **odyssey***

odity   **oddity**

odyssey
There are two *–y*'s in this word, which means "a long, eventful journey." This word comes from the 10-year journey of the Greek warrior Odysseus who was returning from Troy to his home in Ithaca.

oeuvre
This French word is used in English in the expression "**hors d'oeuvre**" and to refer to the work of an artist.

ofense   **offense***

ofer   **offer**

ofering   **offering**

Correct spelling   *Incorrect spelling*

offense

Only a few words end in *–ense*: **defense, dense, expense, immense, intense, pretense, sense, suspense,** and **tense.**

offer, offering

ogel	**ogle**
oger	**ogre***

ogle

ogre

This word for a cruel, oppressive character is probably from a Latin epithet for the god of the underworld, Orcus.

ointment

This word came into Middle English through Old French from the same Latin root that gave us more directly the word **unguent,** *unguentum.* We find the core of **ointment** in the word **anoint,** which was the meaning of the Latin root verb, *unguere.*

omission

omit, omitted, omitting

Because the accent is on the last syllable of **omit,** double the last consonant before adding the suffixes *–ed* and *–ing.*

ommision	**omission***
ommit	**omit***
ommited	**omitted***
ommitting	**omitting***

omnipotent

This is a Latin word for "all-powerful": *omni* (all) and *potent* (powerful).

omniscient

This word for "all knowing" is from Latin, from the same root word as **science.**

onerous

This word is from the Latin word, *onus* (burden or load), a word that we also use in English.

opacity

Correct spelling	*Incorrect spelling*

opaque

opasity   **opacity**

opera

operate

opertunity   **opportunity***

ophthalmologist, ophthalmology
   These words come from the Greek *ophthalmos* (eye). Fortunately
   for poor spellers, we use the easier Greek word *optos* (visible) in
   such words as **optometry** and **optometrist**.

opinion, opinionated

oportunity   **opportunity***

oportunistic   **opportunistic***

opose   **oppose***

oposite   **opposite***

opossum
   We borrowed this word for the common nocturnal, arboreal
   marsupial from Powhatan, the language of Native American tribes
   formerly inhabiting eastern Virginia.

oppera   **opera**

opperate   **operate**

opportunity, opportunistic
   Here's a mnemonic to help you spell these words: "A *port* in a
   storm can lead to a great op*port*unity."

oppose, opposite, opposition
   To remember the two *p*'s, just think of two being necessary to
   keep apart the **opposing** *o*'s.

oppress, oppression, oppressive

oppulence   **opulence**

oppulent   **opulent**

opress   **oppress**

opression   **oppression**

opressive   **oppressive**

| **Correct spelling** | *Incorrect spelling* |

Incorrect spelling	Correct spelling
opthamologist	**ophthalmologist***
opthamology	**ophthalmology***

optical, optician, optics

optimal

optimist, optimism, optimistic
> These words come through French from the Latin *optimus* (best). An **optimist** hopes for and expects the best.

optimum

optometrist, optometry

opulence, opulent

oragin	**origin**
oraginal	**original**

oral/aural (see entry for **aural/oral**)

orange
> This color comes from the Sanskrit word *naranga*, which meant "orange tree."

orbit, orbital, orbiting

orchestra
> Although **orchestra** now means "a group of instrumental musicians," this Greek word once meant "pavilion for dances." To spell it correctly, remember there's a –*chest*– in the middle of the word.

ordinance

o revoir	**au revoir***

organic

origin, original

orkestra	**orchestra***

ornament, ornate

ornery
> This word, which is a corruption of the word **ordinary**, now means "stubborn."

ornge	**orange***

Correct spelling	*Incorrect spelling*

orrigin	**origin**
orriginal	**original**

orthodox

This word is easier to spell if you remember that the only vowel is *o*.

orthopedic, orthopedics, orthopedist

These words, which all have something to do with bones, come from the Greek words *orthos* (straight) and *pais* (child).

oscillate

ostensible

ostentatious

osteopath, osteopathy

osteoporosis

The first half of this word, *osteo*, comes from the Greek word for "bone." In the second half we recognize a relative of the word **porosity**.

ostracism, ostracize

These words come from the Greek, meaning "to banish."

ottoman

Combine the name *Otto* with the word *man* to spell this synonym of footstool. The word comes from French, which borrowed the Arabic word for "Turkish," *othmani*.

ourve	**oeuvre***

outrageous

oval

ovary, ovarian

ovel	**oval**
overraught	**overwrought**

overrule

When two words are combined and the first word ends in the same letter with which the second word begins, both letters stay, which is why you'll find a *–rr–* in the middle of this word.

Correct spelling   *Incorrect spelling*

overrun

overry	**ovary**
overule	**overrule***
overun	**overrun**

overwhelm

overwrought

overy	**ovary**
ownerous	**onerous***

oxymoron

> This word is from a Greek word meaning "pointedly or shrewdly foolish." Because that root combined the words for "sharp" and "foolish," the resulting word, **oxymoron,** came to be used for any linking of two contradictory words.

oyntment, oyntmint	**ointment***

pachyderm

This word for an elephant comes from the Greek words *pachys*, "thick," and *derma*, "skinned."

pacifism, pacifist

package

pageant

Combine the words *page* and *ant* for a word that in the Middle Ages meant "stage" or "scene from a play" and now means "elaborate show."

paid

pail/pale

A **pail** is a bucket. **Pale** means "lacking color" or "to become lighter or less important." It can also be a stake in a fence or refer to limits or bounds.

pair/pare/pear

A **pair** is two of something or to form a twosome. To **pare** is to remove the outside of something or to reduce gradually. A **pear** is a fruit.

pajamas

This word comes from Persian, meaning "loose-fitting trousers."

pakaderm   **pachyderm***

palace

palacial   **palatial**

palate/palette/pallet

These homophones can often be confused. A **palate** is the roof of the mouth or the taste buds. A **palette** is a board used by

---

| **Correct spelling** | *Incorrect spelling* |

artists to mix paint. A **pallet** is a wooden platform is used to support heavy materials.

palatial

pale/pail (see entry for **pail/pale**)

palette/palate/pallet (see entry for **palate/palette/ pallet**)

paliative   **palliative**

pallet/palate/palette (see entry for **palate/palette/ pallet**)

pallette   **palate/palette/ pallet***

palliative

palltry   **paltry**

palpable

paltry

pamphlet

This word comes from the Greek, meaning "loved by all." This word originated in the 1100s for a collection of short love poems. Now it means an unbound publication.

panacea

This word comes from the Greek words *pan* (all) and *akos* (cure). Remember how to spell it by visualizing a *pan* with an *ace* of sp*a*des in it.

panache

This French word came from the Latin for "feather."

pandemonium

This word first appeared in the 1600s in *Paradise Lost*, by John Milton. In the book, Pandemonium was the capital of hell and translated as a place for all demons. Remember how to spell it by finding the **demon** in the middle of this word.

panesea   **panacea***

pantomime

| **Correct spelling** | *Incorrect spelling* |

paradigm

This word comes from two Greek words, *para* (alongside) and *deikunai* (to show). A paradigm is a pattern or example used to establish standards.

paradox, paradoxical

Incorrect spelling	Correct spelling
parafanalia	**paraphernalia***
paralell	**parallel***
paralize	**paralyze**

parallel

Remember the *–all* in the middle of **parallel** with this mnemonic: "Draw *all* of the lines par*all*el."

paralyze, paralysis

paraphernalia

This Greek word meant items of property, such as clothing, personal goods, and gifts that the law allowed a married woman to keep after her dowry was paid. To correctly spell this word, remember to put *her* in the third syllable.

parcel

parcimonious	**parsimonious**

pare/pair/pear (see entry for **pair/pare/pear**)

parlament	**parliament***
parler	**parlor***

parliament, parliamentary

These words for a legislative body and its procedures come from Old French, from the verb for "to talk."

parlor

One of the few words ending in *–or* rather than *–er*. A **parlor**, which is a room in the house to entertain visitors, once meant a confessional or an audience chamber in a monastery where those from outside the cloister would gather. The word is from the French verb *parler*, meaning "to speak."

parradigm, parradime	**paradigm***
parradox	**paradox**

Correct spelling	*Incorrect spelling*

parrallel	**parallel***
parralyze	**paralyze**
parsamonious	**parsimonious**
parsel	**parcel**
parsimonious	
partial, partiality	
partician	**partition**

participant, participate, participatory

particle

> To spell this word correctly, remember that a tiny *part* of matter is a *part*icle.

particular

partition

pasifism	**pacifism**
pasifist	**pacifist**
pasive	**passive**
pasivity	**passivity**
passifism	**pacifism**
passifist	**pacifist**

passive, passivity

passtime	**pastime**

pasteurize

> Although cows in a field may be a pastoral scene, that's not the root of this word, which comes from the name of the man who invented the process, Louis *Pasteur*.

pastime

pastorize	**pasteurize***
pasttime	**pastime**
pasturize	**pasteurize***
pateo	**patio***

pathetic

pathos

Correct spelling	*Incorrect spelling*

patio
This word comes from the Spanish, meaning "a place."

paucity

paultry   **paltry**

pauper

pausity   **paucity**

pavilion
This word comes from the Old French, meaning "butterfly."
Originally, tents had ornate flaps at their entrances. When open,
the flaps often resembled butterfly wings.

pawper   **pauper**

payed   **paid**

peace/piece
Peace is a lack of war or an atmosphere of tranquility. A **piece** is
a part of something.

peak/peek/pique
These homophones won't confuse you if you remember that a
peak is a mountain top, to **peek** is to get a glimpse of something,
and **pique** means show displeasure or resentment to excite or
arouse (such as curiosity).

pear/pair/pare (see entry for **pair/pare/pear**)

peccadillo

pece   **peace/piece***

pedacure   **pedicure**

pedagogical, pedagogue, pedagogy
These words come from the Greek, referring to a slave who
would lead children from home to school and back again. Now
the words refer to educators and education in general.

pedal/peddle
The first of these homonyms is part of a bike or to ride a bike,
while the second is to sell from no fixed location. You can remember that **pedal** ends in *–al* as does the **metal** from which it's
made and you can think of the *–dd-* in **peddle** as standing for
door to **d**oor.

| Correct spelling | *Incorrect spelling* |

pedant, pedantic, pedantry

pedastal   **pedestal**

peddle/pedal (see entry for **pedal/peddle**)

pedestal

pedicure

pedjorative   **pejorative**

pedophile, pedophilia

These words come from Greek roots, *pedo* (child) and *philia* (love).

peer/pier

A **peer** is an equal or to look searchingly. A **pier** is a structure built on posts over water.

peeramid   **pyramid**

peir   **peer/pier***

pejorative

pelpable   **palpable**

penance

penant   **pennant***

penatent   **penitent**

Combine the words *pen* and *i* and *tent* or you'll be sorry when you misspell the word.

penchant

This word comes from the French meaning "to incline." Combine the words *pen* and *chant* to get **penchant**, which means a strong like or inclination.

pencil

pendant

This is one of four words ending in either *–ant* or *–ent* depending whether they're used as a noun or an adjective. (This distinction is changing with usage.) The nouns are **dependant, descendant, pendant,** and **propellant**. The adjectives are **dependent, descendent, pendent,** and **propellent**.

Correct spelling	*Incorrect spelling*

Correct spelling	Incorrect spelling

penecilin, penecillin → **penicillin**

penence → **penance**

penesillin → **penicillin**

penicillin

penitent

pennance → **penance**

pennant

Remember the –nn– in the middle of this word, which is a narrow flag used by a military unit or for a sports team.

pennicillin, pennisillin → **penicillin**

pennitent → **penitent**

pensil → **pencil**

percalate → **percolate**

percent, percentile

perceptive

percolate

perennial

You'll spell this word right if you remember that there will forever be a –nn– in this word.

performance

periphenalia → **paraphernalia***

perjure, perjury

perkolate → **percolate**

Although **percolate** is often shortened to **perk**, the long form is spelled with a c, as in **coffee**.

permanent

permisable → **permissible**

permision → **permission**

permissible

permission

Correct spelling	Incorrect spelling

pernicious

This word comes from the Latin meaning "to kill, harm, or cause injury or destruction."

perogative   **prerogative**

perooze   **peruse***

perpetrator

This mnemonic offers a bit of humor: "The **perpetrator** lost his *pet rat* at the scene of the crime."

perpetual, perpetuate

A friend thinks this mnemonic for **perpetuate** is a groaner, but useful: "It was the *pet (yo)u ate* that gave you the upset stomach."

perquisite

Drop the *p-* and change the *–r* to *–x* and you will have made an *exquisite* profit beyond your salary with all of your **perquisites**.

perrogative   **prerogative**

persent   **percent**

Remember the **cent** in this word, which comes from the Latin word *centum*, "hundred," a word that also gives us **century** and **centennial**.

perseverance

This word is the one exception to the rule that nouns formed from verbs ending in *–ere* will end in *–ence*.

persevere, persevered

The only vowel in these words is an *–e* and the penalty for missing it in *persevere* and *persevered* is *severe*.

persist, persistent

persnickety

persona non grata

This term is pure Latin for an unacceptable person, especially a diplomat caught spying on the host nation.

personal, personify, personification

personnel

This word is French for "personal": we've kept the *–nn-* and the *–e*.

Correct spelling   *Incorrect spelling*

perspective/prospective

These related words, although not really homophones, can be confusing. **Perspective** (*per* is Latin for "through") is a point of view or a view that conveys the effect of distance or depth, while **prospective** (*pro* is Latin for "forward") means looking into the future or anticipating something.

perspire, perspiration

persuade, persuasion, persuasive

persuance	**pursuance**
persuant	**pursuant**
persue	**pursue**

perturb

peruse, perusal

These words come from a Middle English verb meaning "to use up," as if we could "use up" the meaning of words that we read or examine with care. The Latin prefix *per-*, as used in **peruse**, is an intensifier, used also with that effect in such words as **perfect, persuade, pertain, perturb,** and **pervert.**

perview	**purview**
pese	**peace/piece***

pesticide

This word is one of a series of "death nouns"—**suicide, homicide, genocide, herbicide, insecticide,** and so on. The root of all of these words is the same Latin verb, *cadere* (to cut), as we find in **decide, precise,** and **concise.**

peticure	**pedicure**

petulant

phantom

pharmaceutical, pharmaceutics, pharmacy

These words come from the Greek for individuals who made potions and cures as well as poisons and aphrodisiacs. When spelling them, keep in mind that the Greeks had no *f* in their alphabet, only a letter that was later transcribed as *ph*.

Correct spelling   *Incorrect spelling*

phenom
This word is slang for a person who is **phenomenal**.

phenomena, phenomenal, phenomenon
The word **phenomenon** is Greek, which is why the plural is **phenomena**, just as the plural of **criterion** is **criteria**. A friend likes to remember the spelling of these words with this mnemonic: "In these words you'll find *no men*."

philanderer, philandering
These words come from the Greek for "lover of men"—a meaning that has shifted with usage.

philanthropic, philanthropy

phlegm
You'll find a *leg* in this word, although **phlegm** is found only in the respiratory system. **Phlegm** relates to medieval physiology called the humors, which consisted of four fluids: blood, bile, phlegm, and black bile. These humors made people sanguine, bilious, phlegmatic, or melancholy.

phlegmatic
This word describes people who, according to medieval physiology, had an excess of phlegm. When phlegm was the dominant fluid, the individuals were considered to be dull.

photography, photographer, photographic
These words are formed from two Greek roots, *phot-* and *graphein,* to mean "writing with light."

photosynthesis

physical, physically

physician
This individual is legally qualified to practice medicine, once known as the Latin term *physica.*

pianeer   **pioneer***

picayune
This word means a piece of Spanish money worth about a nickel, something of little value. It came to English from the French for a copper coin, a word that came from the Latin word for "money." Now **picayune** means "paltry, petty, or trifling."

| **Correct spelling** | *Incorrect spelling* |

picnic, picnicked, picnicking

This word comes from the French, meaning a pleasant pastime. Part of the word's origin seems to be "to pick a little, to trifle a bit, perhaps to nap." Adding a –k keeps the final hard –c sound of **picnic** in **picnicked** and **picnicking**. Words ending in –c often add a –k before suffixes beginning with –e, –i, or –y, as with **panic**, which takes a k to form **panicked, panicking** and **panicky**.

piece/peace (see entry for **peace/piece**)

pier/peer (see entry for **peer/pier**)

piese   **peace/piece***

pieus   **pious**

piña colada

This Spanish term means "strained pineapple," but don't forget to add the coconut juice and rum when making the beverage.

pinnacle

pioneer

This word is from Old French for "foot soldier" and, before that, Latin for "one with big feet." Pioneers were often sent out ahead of the main body of troops to clear the way. A pioneer ventures into an unknown region and opens the way for others to follow.

pious

pire   **pyre***

pirouette

pistil/pistol

How can you use these homophones correctly? Remember that a **pistil** is part of a plant that produces seeds. The word comes from the Latin for "pestle," from its shape, which is not unlike the *i* in the final syllable of **pistil**. A **pistol** is a small, hand-held firearm. The word comes from Czechoslovakian for "pipe." Look into the barrel of this "pipe" and you'll be reminded of the *o* in the final syllable of **pistol**.

pistol/pistil (see entry for **pistil/pistol**)

pitiful, pity

pius   **pious**

Correct spelling   *Incorrect spelling*

pixel
> This is a new word recently created for the tiny elements that make up an image on a TV or video display unit. *Pix-* stands for picture, *–el* for element.

pizazz or **pizzazz**

pizza

pizzaria   **pizzeria**

pizzazz (or pizazz)

pizzeria

placard

placate

placcard   **placard**

placebo
> This word is Latin for "I shall please." A **placebo** is palliative medicine given to a please a patient who feels a need for medicine. The root *place-* in **placebo** is found in other "pleasing" words, such as **complacent** and (slightly altered) **placate** and **placid**.

placque   **plaque**

plad   **plaid***

plagiarize
> This word comes from a Latin word meaning "to plunder" or "to kidnap." Usage has narrowed the meaning considerably.

plaid
> Remember how to spell this word for a Tartan patterned fabric with this mnemonic: "Each clan had a distinctive **pl*aid***, to *aid* in identifying the origin of the wearer."

plaintiff

plaquard   **placard**

plaque

platitude, platitudinous

plausible
> This word originally meant "deserving applause," used to describe something that seemed likely, possible, or even just impressive.

Correct spelling	*Incorrect spelling*

playwright
The spelling of this word confuses many people, because they think of someone who **writes** plays. But the second half of this word comes from *wright* (a word that no longer exists except as a name): a *wright* was someone who crafted things, such as a **wheelwright** or a **wainwright** (wagons). So, a **playwright** is someone who crafts plays.

pleasant, pleasantries, pleasantry
ploy
plum/plumb
A **plum** is a fruit or an informal variant spelling of **plumb** used as an adjective. **Plumb** can be an adjective (vertical or absolute), a noun (a weight used to determine a true vertical), or a verb (to work as a plumber, to test alignment with a weight, or to determine a depth).

plumb/plum (see entry for **plum/plumb**)
plumbing

plumet	**plummet***
plumeting	**plummeting***
pluming	**plumbing**

Unless you mean the act of decorating with feathers or of taking pride in an accomplishment, you probably mean **plumbing**, as in pipes or working with pipes.

plummet, plummeting
There is an *–mm-* in these words, which mean to drop straight down like lead, which is *plumbum* in Latin. The *–b-* in the root word later lost its pronunciation, so it dropped from the spelling of **plummet**, although it remained in **plumb, plumber**, and **plumbing**.

plumming	**plumbing**

plural
plush
pneumatic
The root of this word is Greek, *pneumon* (lung). Here it's part of a word that describes machines that run on or use compressed air.

Correct spelling	*Incorrect spelling*

pneumonia

The name for this disease comes from the Greek word for lung, *pneumon*.

poignant, poignancy

The pronunciation of these words makes it difficult to remember the *–gn–* combination of letters. The words come from a Latin verb *pungere*, meaning "to sting," which is also the origin of **puncture** and **pungent.** But as the words developed through Old French, the middle consonants became reversed, so we find the same *–gn–* as in such words as **indignant, pregnant,** and **repugnant.**

poinsettia

This plant is named for a diplomat, Joel Roberts Poinsett, who as special minister to Mexico brought the **poinsettia** back to the U.S.

poliethelene	**polyethylene**
polip	**polyp***

politesse

political/politico

These related words, although not true homophones, can be confusing to spell. **Political** is concerned with the administration of government or pertaining to public policy. A **politico** is another term for a **politician.**

politician, politics

politico/political (see entry for **political/politico**)

pollip	**polyp***
pollitical	**political***
pollitician	**politician**
pollitics	**politics**

poltergeist

This word for a ghost or spirit that makes itself known by noise or by moving objects comes from the Greek *poltern* (to make a noise) and *geist* (spirit).

poltry	**poultry**

polyethylene

Correct spelling	*Incorrect spelling*

polyp

Remember the correct spelling here by combining *poly-* with a *–p* to get this word, meaning a growth. The word came into English from French, borrowed from a Latin word with Greek origins, *polypus*, meaning "octopus," literally "many (*poly*) feet."

pontificate

This word means to act pompous or dogmatic, to act like a **pontiff**—the term for a pope, a bishop, or a high priest in ancient Rome.

poor/pore/pour

These homophones won't trip you up if you remember that **poor** means having little means of support or lacking in quality, a **pore** is a small opening in the skin or membrane or to study carefully, and the verb **pour** means to cause to flow.

poorly

poorous	**porous**
popurri	**potpourri***

porcelain

This word comes from a Italian word meaning "little pig." The white, hard, translucent ceramic ware resembles a cowry shell, which the Italians thought resembled a sow's womb.

pore/pour/poor (see entry for poor/pore/pour)

porosity

porous

portfolio

We get this word from Italian, where it was a combination of two words meaning "sheet" and "carry," for a case for holding loose sheets of papers or other materials.

porus	**porous**
posess	**possess***
posessed	**possessed***
posession	**possession***
posessor	**possessor***
posible	**possible***

Correct spelling	*Incorrect spelling*

posibility
possibility*

possess, possessed, possession, possessor

You **possess** the skill to remember that there are two sets of –ss in these words.

possible, possibility

It's **possible** to forget the –ss-, but it wouldn't be correct. This word comes from the same Latin root as *posse*.

posthumous

potato, potatoes

Despite its Irish heritage, this vegetable comes from the Andes region in South America. Remember: every **potato** has eyes, but in the plural **potatoes** also have **toes**.

potpourri

This word is a French translation of the Spanish *olla podrida*, literally "rotten pot," a pungent name for a stew of highly seasoned meats and vegetables. The word was first used in English for a meat stew. Now it has a very different meaning: fragrant dried herbs and flowers used to perfume a room.

poultry

pour/poor/pore (see entry for poor/pore/pour)

practical, practicality, practically

practice

practitioner

pragmatic, pragmatically, pragmatism

These words come from the Greek for "to do" and characterize an approach that is practical.

prairie

Remember the tricky –ai- vowel combination in the middle of **prairie** with this mnemonic: "There's lots of *air* blowing through the pr*ai*rie."

pralude   **prelude***

pray/prey

Don't get caught on these homophones. To **pray** means to say a prayer, while **prey** is the action or goal of a predator.

Correct spelling   *Incorrect spelling*

precapice   **precipice**

precede/proceed

> While these aren't true homophones, they can be tricky. **Precede** means to come before or to take **precedence**. It's is one of only seven words ending in –*cede*. (The others are **antecede, cede, concede, intercede, recede,** and **secede.**) **Proceed** means "to go forward," as in **procedure**. It's one of only three verbs in English that end in –*ceed*. (The other two are **exceed** and **succeed.**)

precedence, preceding

precipice

precise, precision

> **Precise** comes from the Latin meaning "to shorten." We also find the root, –*cis*- (cut) in **concise** and **decisive**, for example.

precocious

> Though this Latin word originally meant to cook beforehand and then referred to plants that flowered early, it now refers to a child who is unusually forward or mature—an early bloomer, we might say, although not precooked.

predator

prefer, preferred, preference, preferential

> Some people get confused between –*r*- and –*rr*- in words built on **prefer**. It's easy: double the final –*r* before adding a suffix if the accent will remain on the final syllable of the word.

prejudice, prejudicial

> The root of these words is from the Latin for "before judgment." To remember how to spell **prejudice** correctly, here's a mnemonic: "Avoiding **preju***dice*, the judge rolled the *dice* to see if the criminal would serve time." As for **prejudicial**, it contains the familiar word **judicial**.

prekoshush   **precocious***

prelude

> This word comes from Latin, meaning "to come before a play or a game."

premier/premiere

> Remember these homophones by recalling that **premier** means

---

Correct spelling   *Incorrect spelling*

"first or foremost" or it's a political title, while **premiere** is the first performance of a play or other event.

premiere/premier (see entry for **premier/premiere**)

preparation, preparatory

preponderance

This word comes from a Latin verb meaning "to have greater weight," a root that also gives us **ponder** (to weigh) and **ponderous** (heavy).

prepparation	**preparation**
prepparatory	**preparatory**

prequel

This word was invented by Hollywood and the media to mean a film, TV show, or book about an earlier stage of a story or characters that have already been the subject of a work. Since **sequel** comes (through Middle English and Old French) from the Latin *sequi*, meaning "to follow," to the Latin purist **prequel** would mean something like "that which follows in advance."

prerequisite

prerogative

presapice	**precipice**

prescience

You'll know in advance how to spell this word if you combine *pre* and *science* for a word that means having knowledge of events before they happen.

prescient

prescipice	**precipice**

prescribe, prescription

presipice	**precipice**

prestidigitation

This word is from the Latin meaning "nimble fingers," thus trick or deceit. The Italians used this word for a magician whose hand was faster than the eye.

Correct spelling *Incorrect spelling*

prestige, prestigious

These words came from a Latin word meaning "full of dazzling tricks." Now they refer to having an importance based on reputation or past achievements.

presume, presumption, presumptuous

pretense

Besides **pretense**, only a few words in American English end in —ense: **defense, dense, expense, immense, intense, offense, sense, suspense,** and **tense**.

pretentious

prevail

prevalent

prey/pray (see entry for **pray/prey**)

primeval

principal/principle

Don't confuse these homophones. **Principal** as a noun is the head or key person in an organization. As an adjective, it means primary or chief. To use this word correctly, remember the mnemonic: "The princi**pal** is my *pal*." A **principle** is a basic rule. To spell it correctly, think of the final —*le* as representing the —*le* in ru*le*.

principle/principal (see entry for **principal/principle**)

prissy

pristine

privacy, private

privilege

A **privilege** may give you an edge, but don't spell it with one. The word comes from two Latin words meaning "private law" (a law affecting only one person); the final syllable has the same root as *legal* and *legitimate*.

proactive

To spell **proactive** correctly, remember this mnemonic: "The *pro* was *active* in rehearsing his lines."

probable, probably

In Middle English, **probable** meant "provable," from the Latin, *prob-*

Correct spelling   *Incorrect spelling*

abilis, which came from the same root as **probe** and **probate**.

procede   **proceed**

procedure

proceed/precede (see entry for **precede/proceed**)

proceedure   **procedure**

proclivity

procrastinate, procrastination, procrastinator
    These words are from Latin, meaning "to postpone or delay."
    Originally the words meant "forward to tomorrow."

prodigal

prodigious
    This word now means impressive, extraordinary, or ominous—the
    last meaning being the original of the Latin root *prodigiosus*.

prodigy

profalactic   **prophylactic**

profesor   **professor***

profession, professional

professor, professorial
    A **professor**, at least originally, was someone who **professed**,
    that is, who claimed knowledge of something.

profilactic   **prophylactic**

prognosis
    This word is pure Greek, meaning "foreknowledge." This word has
    the same Greek root, *gnosis* (knowledge), as we find in **diagnosis**
    and **agnostic**.

prognosticate, prognostication, prognosticator

prohibative   **prohibitive**

prohibit, prohibition

prohibitive

promanence   **prominence**

promanent   **prominent**

promasory   **promissory**

Correct spelling   *Incorrect spelling*

promice   **promise**

prominence, prominent

promiscuous

This word originally meant "all mixed up," from a Latin verb, *miscere*, that gives us **miscellaneous** and **mix.** Over time the meaning evolved to "lacking standards of selection." But now we usually use it to mean "indiscriminate in sexual relations."

promise

promissory

pronounce, pronunciation

propel, propellant

Propellant is one of four words ending in either *–ant* or *–ent* depending whether they're used as an adjective or a noun. (This distinction is changing with usage.) The nouns are **dependant, descendant, pendant,** and **propellant.** The adjectival forms are **dependent, descendent, pendent,** and **propellent.**

prophylactic

propiatary   **proprietary**

propiator   **proprietor**

propitious

This word comes almost unchanged from the Latin word for "favorable" or "auspicious." Spell it right by putting a *pit* in the middle of pro**pit**ious.

proportion, proportional, proportionate

proprietary, proprietor

propulsion

prospective/perspective (see entry for **perspective/ prospective**)

prosthesis, prosthetic

protacal, protacol   **protocol***

protean

This word meaning "able to take on different sizes and shapes," comes from Proteus, a Greek sea god who could change his shape at will.

| **Correct spelling** | *Incorrect spelling* |

proteen	**protein**

protégé(e)

This word is straight French, meaning "protected," and is used to mean someone who is helped, mentored, or otherwise protected by someone. When we distinguish between the two forms, **protégé** and **protégée**, the former is for a man and the latter is for a woman.

protein

protocol

You'll spell **protocol** correctly if you remember that −o is the only vowel in this word.

provadence	**providence***
provadencial	**providential***
provadent	**provident***
provalone	**provolone**
provedance	**providence***
provedant	**provident***
provedencial	**providential***
provence	**province***
provencial	**provincial***

providence, provident, providential

Just remember that we count on **providence** to **provide** and you'll spell these words right.

province, provincial

It's **Provence** with an e (and a capital *P*) only for the southern part of France—and the adjective is **Provençal**.

provocative, provoke

provolone

proxie	**proxy***

proximate

This adjective and the related word **approximate** come from the Latin adjective for "closest" or "nearest."

Correct spelling   *Incorrect spelling*

proximity

proxy

This word came into Middle English from an Old French legal term meaning "care taken of something."

pseudonym, pseudonymous

These words are from Greek, *pseudes* (false) and *onoma* (name).

psyche

Psyche was a Greek maiden who was loved by Eros. After years of tribulations, the two were united, and Psyche was given a place among the gods as the personification of the soul. **Psyche** is defined as something that symbolizes the human soul—anything not flesh and blood.

psychedelic

This word comes from two Greek words and means "mind manipulating." It was probably coined by Dr. Timothy Leary and his colleague, Dr. Richard Alpert, who promoted the use of LSD.

psychiatric, psychiatrist

Both of these words have as their root **psyche**, which comes from the Greek word for "mind" or "soul."

psycho

This word is a colloquial shortening of **psychopath** or **psychotic**.

psychoanalysis, psychoanalytical

Combine the words *psycho* and *analysis* to get a system of psychotherapy developed by Sigmund Freud.

psychological, psychologist, psychology

These words come from Greek words for "mind" and "study."

psychopath

psychoses, psychosis

These words from Greek follow Greek rules: *–is* is singular, *–es* is plural.

psychosomatic

This word is from the Greek words for "mind" and "body." It refers to the interrelation between mind and body as it relates to disease.

psychotic

| Correct spelling | *Incorrect spelling* |

pterodactyl

You can more easily remember the spelling of this prehistoric flying creature if you know that the name was a Latin creation from two Greek words, *pteron* (wing), a root that we also find (with the *p* pronounced) in **helicopter**, and *daktulos* (finger), a root that we also find in … **dactylography** (fingerprinting). (Note that we said only "*more* easily remember"!)

ptomaine

This word is derived from a Greek word, *ptoma*, "corpse." It's logical, since people who get **ptomaine** poisoning often die, especially in centuries past. You might remember the silent *p* if you know that **ptomaine** is caused by the *p*utrefaction of *p*rotein.

puberty, pubescence

publicly

There's a rule that if an adjective ends in *–ic* its adverb form ends in *–ally*. This is the only exception to the rule.

pugnacious

pulmonary

This root of this word is Latin, *pulmo* (lung).

pumpkin

This word is related to **pompon**, a word we get from the Old French word for **pumpkin**. To spell the name of this orange vegetable correctly, combine the words *pump* and *kin*.

punctual, punctuality

pundit

This word is a rare borrowing from Hindi, where it means "a learned person."

purjure	**perjure**
purjury	**perjury**
pursevere	**persevere***
pursist	**persist**
pursistent	**persistent**
pursnickety	**persnickety**
pursuade	**persuade**

Correct spelling	*Incorrect spelling*

Incorrect spelling	Correct spelling
pursuasion	**persuasion**
pursuasive	**persuasive**

pursue, pursuant, pursuance

purturb	**perturb**
puruse	**peruse***

purview

putrefy

Only four verbs end in *–efy*; all the rest end in *–ify*. The other three are **liquefy, rarefy,** and **stupefy. Putrefy** comes from the same Latin root as **putrid** and (through the French) **potpourri.**

puzzle

Puzzle will baffle, mystify, or confuse you if you don't include a –zz– in the middle. By the way, very appropriately, the origin of this word remains a **puzzle.**

pyramid

pyre

This word comes almost directly from a Latin word for "fire," a root we also find in **pyromaniac** and **pyrotechnics,** as well as several dozen erudite words.

pyromaniac

The first part of this word is from a Latin word for "fire" that we find in funeral **pyre** and **pyrotechnics.** The rest of the word is only too familiar!

pyrotechnics

Correct spelling	*Incorrect spelling*

qeeche **quiche***

quagmire

Etymologists are in a linguistic **quagmire** over the first half of this word because its origin is unknown. Remember how to spell it by noting that in all English words, except **Iraq**, the *q* is followed by a *u*.

quaint

qualify, qualification

quality, qualitative

qualm

quandary

This word comes from Latin and means a state of perplexity or indecision in the presence of several acceptable solutions.

quantify, quantification

quantity, quantitative

quantum

This word is pure Latin, a word meaning "how much" or "how great."

quarantine

This word comes from the Italian for "40 days." It was common practice to keep a ship waiting 40 days in the harbor if there was any sign of illness on board, to prevent those who might have been ill from coming ashore and spreading a contagious disease.

quark

Physicists borrowed this word for a hypothetical particle of matter that carries an electrical charge from James Joyce, who coined the word in his book, *Finnegan's Wake*.

| **Correct spelling** | *Incorrect spelling* |

quarry

quartz

quary **query, quarry**

quash

quasi

This word is pure Latin, meaning "as if."

queasy

Remember how to spell this word with this mnemonic: "It's **qu**ite **easy** for your stomach to feel **queasy**."

Quebec

queezen **cuisine***

quintessence

querulous

This word comes from the same Latin root as **query**.

query

questionable, questionnaire

queue/cue (see entry under **cue/queue**)

queuing

quibble, quibbled, quibbling

The experts disagree about the origin of these words, although the root seems to be in the Latin *quibus* (to whom, by whom, for whom, etc.), a word that was found throughout legal documents.

quiche

Although this word is French, it originally came from a German word for "cake."

quiet/quite

While these words aren't true homophones, they're close enough to be confusing. **Quiet** means "peaceful, with little or no noise," while **quite** means "completely, to a great extent."

quintessence, quintessential

quintuple

| Correct spelling | *Incorrect spelling* |

quirk

This word for a personal peculiarity is **quirky** in that the origin is unknown.

quisical   **quizzical**

quisine   **cuisine***

quite/quiet (see entry for **quiet/quite**)

quixotic

This word was coined from Miguel de Cervantes' work, *Don Quixote de la Mancha*, and refers to visionary or eccentric endeavor.

quiz, quizzes, quizzical

quorum

quota

rabid, rabies

These words are from the Latin verb meaning "to rave," which is also the origin of **rage**.

rack/wrack

The **rack** was an instrument of torture where the body was stretched. Now, instead of our bodies, all we usually **rack** is our brains. **Wrack,** as in "bringing to wrack and ruin," is related to **wreck** and derived from an Old English word meaning "punishment."

racket, racketeer

The word **racket** comes from the Arabic, meaning the "palm of the hand." The experts don't know, however, how the meaning of **racket** as noise or illegal business, as in the word **racketeer**, originated.

raconteur

This word is French, from the verb meaning "to recount," and refers to someone who tells stories.

radar

This word is an acronym for *ra*dio *d*etecting *a*nd *r*anging.

radiant, radiate, radiation, radiator

These words come from the Latin *radius*, which is also the origin of **radius**, of course, and **ray**.

radical

This word, from the Latin word for "root," means "pertaining to the root or origin" as well as "drastic." **Radical** shares its root with the word **radish**, a particular root.

rain/reign/rein

These homophones won't give you trouble if you remember that **rain** is condensed water drops falling from the sky, **reign** means

---

Correct spelling   *Incorrect spelling*

"to rule" or "the length of a sovereign's rule," and **rein** means "to check or restrain" or "a strap used to control horses."

rair   **rare**

rambunctious

This word comes from the English *rumbustious*, which derived from the Latin *robustus*, meaning "strong" or "of oak."

rancid, rancidity

rappel/repel

While not true homophones, these words can cause confusion. **Rappel** means "to descend using a rope" while **repel** means "to force or drive back" and is the core of **repellent**.

rapsody   **rhapsody***

rare

rarefy, rarefied

Only four verbs end in *–efy*; all the rest end in *–ify*. In addition to **rarefy**, the others are **putrefy, liquefy,** and **stupefy.**

rarity

rashional   **rational***

rashionale   **rationale***

raspberry

This mnemonic might help you remember how to spell this word: "The seeds in the **raspberry** are abrasive, just like the *rasp* file." Or "she gave the **raspberry** so often during the game that her voice began to *rasp*."

rath, rathful   **wrath, wrathful***

rational, rationale

Rational means "consistent with reason." **Rationale** means "basis" or "fundamental reasons or reasoning." This mnemonic might help you spell **rationale**: "To prevent drunkenness, the bar owner decided to *ration* the amount of *ale* served."

ravage

ravenous

When you're **ravenous**, you tend to **rave** about whatever you eat.

Correct spelling   *Incorrect spelling*

ravioli

When we think of **ravioli**, we think of meet and cheese, not vegetables. But this Italian word derived from the Latin word for "turnip."

Incorrect spelling	Correct spelling
ravvage	**ravage**
ravvenous	**ravenous***
ravvioli	**ravioli***
razberry	**raspberry***
reabilitate	**rehabilitate**
reabilitation	**rehabilitation**
reak	**reek/wreak***
reath	**wreath**

rebel

rebellion, rebellious

These words come from the Latin meaning "make war against." That root is also found in the words **belligerent**, **bellicose**, and **antebellum**. Remember the *–ll–* by the word *bell* in the middle of them.

rebuttal

recalcitrant

This word, which means "to be obstinate" or "to not comply," comes from the Latin for "to kick back with the heel."

Incorrect spelling	Correct spelling
reccommend	**recommend***
reccur	**recur***
reccurred	**recurred***
reccurrence	**recurrence***
recurrent	**recurrent***
reccurring	**recurring***

recede

Recede is one of only seven words ending in *–cede*. The others are **antecede**, **cede**, **concede**, **intercede**, **precede**, and **secede**.

| **Correct spelling** | *Incorrect spelling* |

receded, receding

receipt

This word is from Latin, meaning "to receive." Originally **receipt** meant a **recipe** for cooking as well as a prescription for medicine. Contemporary usage has **receipt** meaning "written acknowledgment of payment of money."

receive, receiving

These words are examples of the "*i* before *e* except after *c*" rule.

reception

recess

Recess is a **cessation** of school and comes from the Latin meaning "to yield, move, or withdraw."

recession, recessive

recidivism, recidivist

recieve	**receive***
recieving	**receiving***
recind	**rescind***

recipe

This word is the Latin imperative meaning "take!" It originally meant a set of directions for making a prescription, which is why shorthand for a prescription is Rx. (The slant bar across the base of the R is a sign of the Roman god, Jupiter, the patron of medicines.) In contemporary usage, a **recipe** is a set of cooking directions.

reciprocal, reciprocate, reciprocity

These words are from the Latin meaning "backward and forward."

reckless

recognition, recognize, recognizance

recommend, recommended, recommendation

To spell these words correctly, remember that **commend** is found in all of them.

recur, recurred, recurrence, recurrent, recurring

Despite meaning "to occur again," **recur** has only one *c* and no *o*.

Correct spelling   *Incorrect spelling*

redundant, redundancy

The source of these words is a Latin verb, meaning "to overflow."

reek/wreak

Reek is rooted in Scandavian languages, where it meant "smoke." Now it generally means "to smell (unpleasant)," either literally or figuratively. **Wreak** comes from Old English; the word is related to **wrack** and **wreck** and is usually used only in such expressions as "**wreak** havoc" or "**wreak** revenge."

reeth   **wreath**

refer, reference, referral, referred, referring

Double the last consonant before adding the suffixes *–ed, –al,* and *–ing,* because the accent is on the last syllable of the base word **refer,** but not with suffix *–ence,* because the accent then shifts to the first syllable.

refrigerator

This word comes from the Latin *refrigerans,* which meant "to thoroughly cool." The shortened version of this word *fridge,* is spelled to more closely represent the pronunciation.

regenerate

regime

This French word means "the ruling government" or "the length of its rule." It comes from the Latin word *regimen,* which also gives us, of course, **regimen.**

rehabilitate, rehabilitation

rehearsal

This word comes from a French verb meaning "to harrow over again." And, yes, it's related to **hearse** through a curious, twisted history too long to relate here. Here's a mnemonic to help you remember how to spell it: "During **rehearsal,** the conductor asked the violins to play softly so he could *hear* the flutes."

reign/rein/rain (see entry for **rain/reign/rein**)

rein/reign/rain (see entry for **rain/reign/rein**)

reiterate, reiteration

rejenerate   **regenerate**

| **Correct spelling** | *Incorrect spelling* |

relevance, relevant

remanisce **reminisce**

remembrance

Remember, the word **remember** is not contained in this word.

reminisce, reminiscent

remit, remitted, remittance

The word **remit** originally meant "to send back," but now usually means "to give money for goods and services provided." To spell these words correctly, double the last consonant before adding the suffixes *–ed* and *–ance* because the accent is on the last syllable of the base word **remit**.

remodel, remodeling

remunerate, remuneration

The root in these words is the Latin word *munus* (gift), a root we also find in **munificent**. To **remunerate** means to compensate.

renaissance

This word comes from a Latin verb meaning "to be born again."

rendezvous

It's easy to remember how to spell this French word if you remember *EZ* Street is where you're supposed to meet.

renegade

This word originally meant someone who abandoned his or her religion, i.e., reneged on the commitment to the Catholic Church particularly during the Spanish Inquisition. To remember how to spell **renegade**, think of this mnemonic: "*Egad!* It's a soldier who deserted his platoon."

reoccur **recur**

Many dictionaries don't include *reoccur*, even as a variant spelling for **recur**, although it's in popular usage. It's best to avoid it and use **recur**.

repel/rappel (see entry for **rappel/repel**)

repellent

To spell **repellent**, remember that the only vowel this word contains is *–e*.

| Correct spelling | *Incorrect spelling* |

repent, repentance, repentant

repercussion

This word comes from the Latin word that gives us **percussion**, for instruments that we strike. The *–cuss* in this word is the same as in **discuss**. The *re-* prefix gives **repercussion** the meaning of "striking back"—consequence.

repetition, repetitious, repetitive

It's appropriate that the vowels *–e* and *–i* are repeated in these words that refer to repeating.

reprehensible, reprehensibility

reproach, reproachful

reprobate

This word comes from the Latin verb meaning "reproved," as **probate** comes from the verb meaning "proved."

repudiate

repugnant

requisite, requisition

rescidivism	**recidivism**
rescidivist	**recidivist**

rescind

We get this word from a Latin verb meaning "to cut."

resede	**recede***

resemble, resemblance

reservoir

resilience, resilient

resistable	**resistible**

resistance, resistant

Remember the *–ance* in the final syllable with this mnemonic: "The Surgeon General has expressed strong **resist*ance*** to getting a *tan*."

resistible

responsible, responsibility

Correct spelling	*Incorrect spelling*

ressemblance	**resemblance**
ressemble	**resemble**

restaurant

> **Restaurant**, which comes from the French word for "to restore," has an *aura* in the middle of it, even though not every restaurant's environment has a good aura.

restaurateur

> This word means the manager or owner of a restaurant, although there's no **restaurant** in it.

resterant	**restaurant***
resterater	**restaurateur***

resume, resumption

résumé

> This word is French for "summary": you use a **résumé** to *sum* up your accomplishments. It's sometimes spelled **resume**, without the accent marks.

resuscitate

retaliate, retaliation, retaliatory

> **Retaliate** means "to return like with like," usually in response to a negative incident. The root is the Latin *talio* (punishment in kind), a word that comes into English with the same meaning in **talion**.

reteric	**rhetoric***

reticence, reticent

retoric	**rhetoric***
retreeve, retreive	**retrieve**

retribution

retrieve, retrieval

retroactive, retroactively, retroactivity

revalation	**revelation**
revalatory	**revelatory**
revalie	**reveille***
revarence	**reverence***

Correct spelling   *Incorrect spelling*

revarent   **reverent***

reveal

reveille
> This French word derives from a verb meaning "to awaken or arouse" and is best known as a bugle call to soldiers or campers to rise in the morning.

revel
> Spelling **revel** is easier if you remember that it's **lever** spelled backward. (Of course, if you can't spell **lever**, just spell **revel** in reverse.)

revelation, revelatory

revelie   **reveille***

reverence, reverent
> When spelling these words, the only vowel you'll find is —e and *ever* is in there as well.

reverential

reville   **reveille***

revise
> **Revise** is one of 11 commonly misspelled words ending in *–ise*. The others are **advertise, advise, apprise, chastise, despise, devise, exercise, improvise, supervise,** and **surprise**.

revvelation	**revelation**
revvelatory	**revelatory**
revverence	**reverence***
revverent	**reverent***
revverential	**reverential**

rhapsody
> This word is from a Greek word for "stitched together songs"— appropriate for an instrumental music composition of irregular form. The Greeks also gave us (indirectly) a few other *rh-* words—including **rhetoric, rheumatism, rhinoceros,** and **rhododendron**.

rhetoric
> **Rhetoric** goes back to the ancient Greeks, who gave us both the word and the art of skillful use of language.

Correct spelling	*Incorrect spelling*

rheumatism

If you have **rheumatism**, your joints and muscles are stiff and inflamed. The Greeks created this word to mean "to suffer from rheum."

rhinoceros

Rhino- comes from the Greek word for "nose" and *–ceros* comes from the Greek word for "horn." We find the prefix *rhino-* in the words **rhinology** (medical study of the nose) and **rhinoplasty** (plastic surgery on the nose).

rhododendron

The name of this showy evergreen shrub with clusters of flowers comes from Greek words meaning "rose tree."

rhubarb

The sharp taste of this herb that was originally imported from Russia resembles a *barb*.

rhyme/rime

Rhyme refers to words with similar sounds. **Rime** is a variant spelling of **rhyme**, but it's also a type of frozen precipitation that covers vegetation, a hoarfrost.

rhythem	**rhythm***
rhythemic	**rhythmic**
rhythemical	**rhythmical**

rhythm

When spelling this musical word, the only vowel you'll need is *–y*. But don't forget the two *h's* either.

rhythmic, rhythmical

ricochet

This French word originally meant "endless repetition."

riddle

ridicule, ridiculous

The root of these words is Latin, *ridere* (to laugh), a word that also evolved into **deride**.

rigatoni

This word for pasta made in short wide fluted tubes is Italian, from a word that means "furrowed" or "fluted."

Correct spelling	*Incorrect spelling*

riger	**rigor*, rigueur***
rigerous	**rigorous***

right/rite/write

Right means "correct" or "what is just, legal, or proper" or "something belonging to someone by nature or law." **Rite** is "a religious or otherwise solemn ceremony." **Write** is "the action of putting letters or words into a visual or tactile form or of composing."

rigor, rigorous

Combine *rig* and *or* for these words that come to us unchanged from Latin.

rigueur

The expression **de rigueur** is pure French, "required by fashion or custom, socially obligatory."

rime/rhyme (see entry for **rhyme/rime**)

ring/wring

The first of these homophones can mean "something circular" or "to form something circular" or "to make a noise." The second means "to twist and/or squeeze."

rinoserus	**rhinoceros***
riskay	**risqué***

risotto

This Italian dish consists of rice cooked in broth.

risqué

This word is pure French, the past participle of the verb "to risk," for a particular risk, that of offending a sense of delicacy or propriety.

rissotto	**risotto***

rite/right/write (see entry for **right/rite/write**)

rithm, rithym	**rhythm***

robust

This word comes more or less directly from Latin, where *robustus* meant "strong" or "of oak."

Correct spelling   *Incorrect spelling*

rododendron	**rhododendron***

romanic/romantic

Some people are careless in pronouncing the second of these two words, making them homophones. We almost always mean the second word, which refers to **romance**. The first means "of or derived from the ancient Romans."

roomanate	**ruminate***
roomate	**roommate***
roomatizm	**rheumatism***
roomenate	**ruminate***

roomer/rumor

A **roomer** is "someone who rents a room, a lodger." A **rumor** is "unverified information of uncertain origin."

roominate	**ruminate***

roommate

When two words are combined and the first word ends in the same letter with which the second word begins, you keep both letters—even though you may want to get rid of the **roommate**. This is why you'll find a *–mm-* in the middle of this word.

rootabaga	**rutabaga***

rote/wrote

Rote is "a fixed, habitual, or mechanical course of procedure," as in the expression "by **rote**." **Wrote** is the past tense of **write**.

roulette

This word comes to us from the French meaning "little wheel," the center of this game.

rubarb	**rhubarb***

ruinous

rumanate	**ruminate***
rumer	**roomer/rumor***

ruminate

Originally just a fancy way to say "chew cud," this word now means "to meditate or reflect, to think about."

Correct spelling	*Incorrect spelling*

rumor/roomer (see entry for **roomer/rumor**)

rutabaga

The word for this turnip-like vegetable comes from a Swedish dialectal term that originally meant "root bag." Unfortunately, the roots of this word don't make this root sound any more appetizing.

rythm, rythym   **rhythm***

| *saavy* | **savvy*** |

sabotage

This word comes from the French word *sabot*, meaning "shoe" or "boot."

sac/sack

The first of these words is simply the French version of the second word. However, in English, a **sac** is "a pouch or pouchlike structure in a plant or animal." A **sack** is a bag or a verb meaning "to dismiss from employment" or "to plunder."

saccharin

This word was coined in 1885 for a calorie-free sweetener that is several hundred times sweeter than cane sugar. (If you have trouble spelling this word, you could use the other term for this substance, **ortho-sulfobenzoic acid imide**.)

sachet/sashay

Sachet is "a small packet of perfume used to scent clothes."
Sashay is an old word meaning "to strut or flounce."

sack/sac (see entry for **sac/sack**)

sacrafice	**sacrifice***
sacraficial	**sacrificial***
sacrelege	**sacrilege***
sacreligious	**sacrilegious***

sacrifice, sacrificial

This word is from the Latin "to make sacred." Its meaning has expanded and weakened over the centuries.

sacrilege, sacrilegious

The Latin root, *sacrilegium*, originally meant "theft of sacred things."

| **Correct spelling** | *Incorrect spelling* |

The first part of these words we also find in **sacrifice**. The second part of this word comes from the same verb, *legere* (gather), that evolved into **collect**. There is no linguistic connection between the words **sacrilegious** and **religious**. To spell these words correctly, remember that the word **rile** is found in the middle and that being **sacrilegious** *riles* up those who are religious.

sacurin	**saccharin**
sader	**Seder***

sadism, sadist, sadistic

These words owe their lives to Donatien Alphonse François, the Marquis de Sade, whose sexual escapades involved getting satisfaction by inflicting pain on lovers. His various activities and his writings about them branded his name on this type of behavior.

sail/sale

The first of these homophones refers to a piece of cloth or other fabric used to move a boat. The second is related to the verb **sell**. To remember which is which, think of the *–ai–* in **sail** as in *air*, which moves to make the sail work.

salary/celery (see entry for celery/salary)

sale/sail (see entry for sail/sale)

salmon

This word comes from the Latin *salire*, meaning "to leap." (That verb also evolved into such erudite words as **saltation** and **saltatory** but also into **somersault** and, through French, **sauté**.) Remember the silent *–l–* by thinking of the **salmon** *l*eaping upstream to spawn.

salvage, salvageable

samen, samon	**salmon***
sanatary	**sanitary**
sanatation	**sanitation**
sanaty	**sanity***

sanctimonious

This word comes from a Latin word meaning "sacredness," but now has the negative meaning of being hypocritical or of feigning holiness.

Correct spelling	*Incorrect spelling*

sandwich

This food was created by John Montague, the fourth Earl of Sandwich, in the 18th century. During an all-night card game, Montague became hungry but didn't want to leave the table to eat. His servants brought him meat between two pieces of bread, so his hands would stay clean. So, now we could be calling this food a "Montague."

sanguine

Although this word is from the French for "bloody," it means "having an optimistic temperament or cheerful disposition."
Sanguine relates to the medieval physiology of the four humors: blood, bile, phlegm, and black bile. When blood was the dominant humor, it showed in the complexion and made the person cheerful and passionate.

sanitary, sanitation

sanity

This word and the related adjective **sane** come from the same Latin root, *sanus*, meaning "healthy," as **sanitary** and **sanitation**. Somewhere through the centuries developed a distinction between physical health and mental health. But remembering the common root of all these words may help you keep your **sanity** while spelling them.

sarandipitous	**serendipitous***
sarandipity	**serendipity***

sarcasm, sarcastic

sardine

sarendipitous	**serendipitous***
sarendipity	**serendipity***
sargent	**sergeant***
saringe	**syringe***
sarum	**serum**
sasafras	**sassafras***

sashay/sachet (see entry for **sachet/sashay**)

Correct spelling	*Incorrect spelling*

sasheate, sashiate	**satiate***

sassafras

Sassafras comes to us from the Spanish. Remember the correct spelling by recalling that the flavoring from the leaves of this Eastern North American tree adds a little *sass* to food.

Satan, satanic, satanical, satanism

The base word, **Satan**, has come down through the centuries virtually unchanged from Hebrew, where the root word meant "devil" or "adversary," from the verb form "he accused."

sate, satiate

These two synonyms came into English at different times from the same Latin source, *satis* (sufficient), a word that we find in **satisfy**, a third synonym.

satire, satirical

These words come from a Latin word meaning "mixture." The word **satire** originally meant a long, speech-like poem covering a wide range of subjects including ones that ridiculed and scorned human follies and vices.

sattanic	**satanic***
sattanical	**satanical***

sauna

This Finnish word refers to a steam bath created by throwing water onto hot rocks.

savory

savvy

You'll be well-informed and shrewd if you put a *-w-* in the middle of this word, which is a corruption of the Spanish verb *sabe* (you know).

scaffold

scallion

scallop

sceleton	**skeleton**
scematic	**schematic**
sceme	**scheme**

Correct spelling	*Incorrect spelling*

scenario

This word was borrowed from the Italian with only a change in pronunciation. It comes from a Latin word meaning "of the stage."

scene

scepter

A **scepter** is rod or staff, an emblem of authority, but originally in Greek it was only a lowly staff.

Correct spelling	Incorrect spelling
sceptic	**skeptic***
scepticism	**skepticism***

schedule

This word comes from Latin, *schedula*, "papyrus leaf"—the same **papyrus** that gave us **paper**.

scheme, schematic

schizophrenia, schizophrenic

This psychological term was borrowed recently from the Greek— *schizo* (to split) and *phrenia* (mental disorder).

schmooze

This word comes from the Yiddish meaning "to chat," which derives from the word for "rumor." (An earlier variant of the word used an –s instead of the –z.)

scholar, scholarly

These words come from the Latin word that also gives us **school**.

scintillate

This word comes from Latin, meaning "giving off sparks." The root **scintilla** came into English unchanged in spelling, but meaning "a minute amount." Remember how to spell **scint*ill*ate** by recalling that the word *till* is in the middle.

scion

Scion is one of three nouns that end in –*cion*. The others are **coercion** and **suspicion**. All the rest with the *shun* sound end in –*cian*.

scissors

There's an –*ss* in the middle of this word that's from the Latin, meaning "to cut." We also find the same root in words such as **incisor**.

scolar	**scholar***
scroople	**scruple***
scroopulous	**scrupulous***

scrumptious

To recall how to spell this word, remember this mnemonic: "The guests thought the *rump* roast was **scrumptious** and asked for seconds." (They also didn't care that the word may have derived as an alteration of **sumptuous**.)

scruple, scrupulous

These words come from the Latin for a tiny stone that represented a small unit of weight—an interesting origin for an ethical principle.

scrutinize, scrutiny

The Latin root of these words that means "to search or examine," came from an earlier word for "trash."

scuba

This recent creation is an acronym for "**s**elf-**c**ontained **u**nderwater **b**reathing **a**pparatus."

sculptor, sculpture

Sculptor is one of the few words ending with the suffix *–or*.

sea/see

The first of these homophones designates a large body of water or (figuratively) other substances or objects and the second refers to vision, literally or figuratively.

séance

This French word meaning "meeting" has a narrower sense in English, a meeting for people to receive spiritualistic messages.

seaquel	**sequel***
seaquence	**sequence**
seaquential	**sequential**
seathe	**seethe***

secede

Secede is one of only seven words ending in *–cede*. The others are **antecede, cede, concede, intercede, precede**, and **recede**.

secret

secretarial, secretary

A good **secretary** can keep a **secret**, which was the role of the
medieval Latin *secretarius*, a confidant or a confidential officer.

secrete

This word has two quite different meanings, but they evolved from
the same word. Whether you use **secrete** to mean "to generate a
substance" or to mean "to conceal in a hiding place," the word
comes from a Latin verb meaning "to sever" or "to separate."

secure, security

sedantary	**sedentary***
sedar	**cedar*, Seder***

sedative

sedentary

This word comes from a Latin verb, *sedere*, meaning "to sit." We
also find this root in other words, such as **sedan, supersede,**
and **sediment.**

Seder

This word for the Jewish feast commemorating the exodus of the
Israelites from Egypt is a form of the Hebrew word for "order."

seditive	**sedative**

see/sea (see entry for **sea/see**)

seed/cede (see entry for **cede/seed**)

seege	**siege**
seequel	**sequel***
seequence	**sequence**
seequential	**sequential**

seethe

This word is pure English, dating back to at least before the 12th
century. It formerly was the verb for "boil," but now we use it
only figuratively, such as when our blood boils. Here's a mnemonic
to help you spell it: "You can't always *see* the anger of people who
seethe."

Correct spelling	*Incorrect spelling*

segment

segue

This word comes from the Italian meaning "there follows," and means to move smoothly from one musical selection to another. We also use the Latin equivalent, in the negative, when we label an illogical statement or conclusion a **non sequitur**.

seige   **siege**

seize, seizure

Two of six exceptions to the "*i* before *e* except after *c*" rule. The others are **either, neither, leisure,** and **weird**.

sellabrate   **celebrate**

sellabration   **celebration**

sellabratory   **celebratory**

Companies that try to get us excited about buying their products have also tried to get us to accept these words they've created. Fortunately, they have not succeeded—yet.

seller/cellar (see entry for **cellar/seller**)

semanal   **seminal**

semantic

When we label a discussion as **semantics**, we mean that it's of little or no practical importance. But the Greek root, *semantikos*, meant the opposite—**significant**.

sematary   **cemetery***

Remember the Stephen King novel, *Pet Sematary*? He spelled the word incorrectly for a certain effect. But unless that's your intention, too, here's a mnemonic: start the word with a *ce-* (first and last letters of **corpse**) and put *meter* in the middle (buried two meters deep).

seminal

senario   **scenario***

sene   **scene**

sensability   **sensibility**

sensable   **sensible**

| **Correct spelling** | *Incorrect spelling* |

Incorrect	Correct
sensative	**sensitive**
sensativity	**sensitivity**

sense

Besides **sense**, only a few words in American English end in –ense: **dense, defense, expense, immense, intense, offense, pretense, suspense,** and **tense.**

sensible, sensibility

sensitive, sensitivity

sentament	**sentiment***
sentamental	**sentimental***
sentamentality	**sentimentality***

sentence

Your sentence will be correct if you remember to use only –e as the vowel when spelling the word.

sententious

sentient

sentiment, sentimental, sentimentality

This mnemonic might help you remember how to spell these French words that mean a romantic or nostalgic feeling: "People take *time* to remember when being **sentimental.**" Actually, the Latin root, *sentimentum*, comes from the same verb that gives us **sense** and **sentence.**

separate

Two *a*'s separate the two *e*'s in this word. A friend spells this word by remembering that it starts with *apes* spelled backward. Odd, perhaps, but it works.

separation

septer	**scepter***

septic

sequan	**sequin***

sequel

This word comes from the Latin, meaning "to follow," for something that follows something else.

Correct spelling   *Incorrect spelling*

sequence, sequential

sequin

This word for a small, shiny ornamental disk comes from the name of a gold coin used by the Venetian Republic. The Italian word *zecchino* (coin) passed through French and voilà!—it emerged as **sequin**.

serendipitous, serendipity

These words came from a fairy tale in which the characters, three princes from Serendip (the old name for the country of Sri Lanka), had the ability to make fortuitous or lucky discoveries.

serene, serenity

sergeant

Combine *serge* and *ant* to get this military word, which comes through Old French from the Latin word that gives us **servant**. In Middle English, a **sergeant** was just a common soldier.

serial/cereal (see entry for **cereal/serial**)

sertify   **certify**

serum

serup   **syrup***

sethe   **seethe***

sever/severe

These words are not true homophones, but they often confuse the speller. **Sever** means to cut off or end. You can remember how to spell it by cutting off the last –e in this word. **Severe** means extreme or strict.

severance

Employees receive **severance** pay when their relationship with the employer is **severed**.

severe/sever (see entry under **sever/severe**)

severely

sevrance   **severance***

shalom

When you spell this word, remember to keep a *halo* in the middle. **Shalom** is the Hebrew word for "peace."

Correct spelling   *Incorrect spelling*

shammy	**chamois***
shananigans	**shenanigans***
shapperon	**chaperon** or
	chaperone*
sharif	**sheriff***
shaufeur	**chauffeur***

sheaf, sheaves

shear/sheer

You can see right through these homophones if you remember that **sheer** means "something thin or fine" and **shear** means "to cut or trim." This mnemonic might help: "Don't cut the sheep's *ear* when you **shear** it."

sheer/shear (see entry for **shear/sheer**)

shef	**chef**

sheik/chic (see entry for **chic/sheik**)

shenanigans

This word, with its possible Irish roots, means "mischief" or "I play tricks."

shepherd

This word comes from two Old English words meaning "sheep" and "herdsman."

sherbet

sheriff

This word is from Middle English and once meant the representative of royal authority in a shire.

sherry

shinanigans	**shenanigans***

shine, shining, shiny

shofer	**chauffeur***

shortening

Although we pronounce this word as having two syllables, remember that it has 10 letters and contains the number *ten*. You don't double the *–n* of **shorten** when adding the suffix *–ing* because the accent is not on the last syllable.

Correct spelling	*Incorrect spelling*

| Correct spelling | Incorrect spelling |

sicofant, sicophant   **sycophant***

siege

sieve

To spell this word correctly remember that the word *–eve* ends it.

sifilis   **syphilis**

sifun   **siphon**

sight/cite/site (see entry for **cite/sight/site**)

significant

Spelling this word is easy with the mnemonic, "How will I *sign if I can't* write?"

silable   **syllable***

silhouette

This word comes from a popular European folk art consisting of shadow or outline portraits, named after Louis XV's minister of finance, Etienne de Silhouette.

sillable   **syllable***

sillowet, siloowet, silowet   **silhouette***

simalar   **similar**

simalarity   **similarity**

simaltaneous   **simultaneous**

simbiosis   **symbiosis***

simbiotic   **symbiotic***

simbull   **symbol***

simetrical   **symmetrical***

simetry   **symmetry***

simfoney   **symphony***

similar, similarity

simile

The word *mile* is found in this figure of speech that uses "like" or "as" to compare two different things.

simmetrical   **symmetrical***

simmetry	**symmetry***
simmilar	**similar**
simmilarity	**similarity**
simoltaneous	**simultaneous**
simpathetic	**sympathetic***
simpathy	**sympathy***
simposium	**symposium***
simtom	**symptom**
simultaneous	
sinagogue	**synagogue***
sinc	**sync, synch***
sincere, sincerely, sincerity	
sincronicity	**synchronicity***
sincronize	**synchronize***
syncronous	**synchronous***
sinergism	**synergism***
sinergistic	**synergistic***
sinergy	**synergy***

singe, singeing

Singe is one of two verbs ending in —e that keep the —e when adding the —ing suffix. The other word is **tinge**, which becomes **tingeing**.

singular

sinic	**cynic***
sinical	**cynical***
sinnagogue	**synagogue***
sinnic	**cynic***
sinnical	**cynical***
sinthesise, sinthesize	**synthesize***
sinthetic	**synthetic***

Correct spelling	*Incorrect spelling*

sintillate	**scintillate***
siphon	
siringe	**syringe***
sirloin	
sirop	**syrup***
sirosis	**cirrhosis***
sirup	

A variant spelling of **syrup**.

Sisifus	**Sisyphus***
sisors, sissors	**scissors***
sistem	**system***
sistematic	**systematic***
sistemic	**systemic***

Sisyphus

This word is the name of a cruel Corinthian king who was crafty enough to cheat death twice. However, when he died, as his punishment, he was forced repeatedly to roll a boulder up a hill in Hades only to have it always roll down again when he neared the top.

site/cite/sight (see entry for **cite/sight/site**)

sizzers	**scissors***
skallion	**scallion**
skejule	**schedule***

skeleton

skeptic, skepticism

These words are from the Greek meaning "to look at carefully, to examine." Thus it's only natural to question, doubt, and disagree.

skillful, skillfully

You'll spell **skillfully** skillfully if you remember to put two sets of —lls in it.

sleave	**sleeve**

sleazy

sleeve

Correct spelling	*Incorrect spelling*

smarmy

If you remember there's an *army* in **smarmy,** a word that comes from a dialectal word for "gush" or "slobber," you'll spell it correctly.

smoky

smorgasbord

The Swedish took this word from Old Norse to mean "sandwich table," a place where you can pile things onto an open-faced sandwich. Since we no longer use a slab of bread as a plate, it now means a buffet meal featuring a variety of dishes.

snafu

This word is an acronym for *s*ituation *n*ormal, *a*ll *f*ouled *u*p, which was coined during World War II.

sneak, sneaky, sneakers

soffit

This word for the underside of a part of a building (as of an over-hang or staircase), comes from a French derived from a Latin word meaning "to fasten underneath."

Incorrect spelling	Correct spelling
sofisticate	**sophisticate**
sofisticated	**sophisticated**
sofistication	**sophistication**
sofit	**soffit***
sofmore	**sophomore**

solemn

soliloquy, soliloquies

This Latin word was coined by St. Augustine, meaning "to talk to oneself" or "to speak alone."

solum	**solemn**

sonar

This word is an acronym for *so*und *na*vigation *r*anging.

sophisticate, sophisticated, sophistication

sophomore, sophomoric

This word comes from the Greek meaning "wise fool." A second-year student who has acquired some knowledge tends to exploit it beyond its actual worth, leading to the adage, "a little knowledge is a dangerous thing."

sorbet

sord   **sword**

sordid

sorority

soupe du jour

This word is from the French meaning "soup of the day." We now add **du jour** to various words, to suggest something trendy or short-lived.

spacial   **spatial**

spacific   **specific**

spacifically   **specifically**

spacious

spaghetti

This is an Italian word for "little strings."

spasific   **specific**

spasifically   **specifically**

spatial

spatious   **spacious**

speach   **speech***

special, specially, specialty

These words come through Middle English and Old French from the Latin *species*—just as **general, generally,** and **generality** come through from the Latin *genus*. Centuries later, scientists borrowed both of these words directly from Latin.

specific, specifically, specify

specimen

This word is pure Latin, from the verb *specio*, meaning "to see or look at."

specious

This word comes from a Middle English word meaning "attractive,"

Correct spelling   *Incorrect spelling*

which derives from a Latin word for "appearance." A **specious** argument appears true, but it's actually false.

speech

Although we **speak**, what we produce is **speech**.

Incorrect	Correct
spesific	**specific**
spesifically	**specifically**
spesify	**specify**
spesimen	**specimen***

spinach

No matter what Popeye thinks, this word for a Southeastern Asian plant having edible leaves goes back through Old French and Old Spanish.

spiral

sponsor

This pure Latin word comes from the verb *spondere*, meaning "to pledge," since a **sponsor** assumes responsibility for someone or something. This root also developed into **respond** and **responsibility**.

spurious

This word comes from the Latin for "illegitimate," meaning "counterfeit."

squirrel

The name of this member of the rodent family comes from a Greek word meaning "shadow tail." To spell **squirrel** correctly, remember the *–rr-* (*r*ascally *r*odent?).

stagnant, stagnate, stagnation

The Latin root for these words meant "swamp."

stake/steak

A **stake** can be a sharpened piece of wood, metal, or plastic or some property or an interest, as well as a verb involving one of the preceding nouns. A **steak** is a cut of meat or fish.

stalactite

This is a mineral formation in a cave, hanging from the roof. As

teachers remind their students, "Remember the difference
between a **stalactite** and a **stalagmite**: a **stalactite** must hold
tight to the roof of the cave to avoid falling." So they remember
the difference, but sometimes have trouble spelling both words.

stalagmite
This is a mineral formation in a cave, projecting upward from the
floor. As teachers remind their students, "Remember the difference
between a **stalagmite** and a **stalactite**: a **stalagmite** stands
mighty like a tree." Although that helps you remember the difference, it may confuse you about the spelling of the final syllable.

stationary/stationery
Don't let these homophones stop you in your tracks or freeze
over your sheet of paper. **Stationary** means immobile.
Remember the −*a*- in the ending with the word "st*a*ble."
Stationery is writing materials, such as paper and envelopes. It is
one of two commonly used words ending in −*ery*. The other one
is **cemetery**.

stationery/stationary (see entry for **stationary/
stationery**)

statistics

statuary

statue/statute
While not true homophones, these words can be confused. A
statue is a three-dimensional form or likeness crafted from stone,
clay, wood, or bronze. A **statute** is a law enacted by a legislature.

statue, statuesque

statute/statue (see entry for **statue/statute**)

statute, statutory

steak/stake (see entry for **stake/steak**)

steal/steel
To **steal** is to take without right or permission. **Steel** is a hard
alloy of iron and carbon or to make hard, strengthen.

stealth, stealthy

| **Correct spelling** | *Incorrect spelling* |

steel/steal (see entry for **steal/steel**)

stelacmite	**stalagmite***
stelagtite	**stalactite***

stellar

This word comes from the Latin for "star," *stella.* Here's a mnemonic to help you spell it: "With his son's life at stake, William *Tell* gave a **stellar** performance."

stelth	**stealth**
stelthy	**stealthy**

stench

stimie	**stymie***
stimied	**stymied***

stimulant, stimulate

stimulus, stimuli

Stimulus is pure Latin, which is why the plural ends in *–i.*

stirrup

stolen/stollen

Although not true homophones, these words can be confusing. **Stolen** means to wrongfully take, while **stollen** is a sweet bread containing fruits and nuts.

stollen/stolen (see entry for **stolen/stollen**)

stomach

This word for one of the organs in the digestive system is from the Greek for "mouth." This word sometimes confuses when it grows into **stomachache**.

store, storage

straight/strait

These homophones won't confuse you if you remember that **straight** is usually an adjective, meaning not curved or bent, while **strait** is a noun, for a narrow passageway connecting two large bodies of water or a position of difficulty or distress.

straight-laced	**strait-laced**

Correct spelling   *Incorrect spelling*

strait/straight (see entry for **straight/strait**)

straitjacket

This garment is used to restrain the arms of a violent person tightly against their body. The term comes from a meaning of **strait** as constructed or bound tightly.

strait-laced

strategic, strategy

strength, strengthen

Although we don't pronounce the –g– in these words, we don't forget it when we remember that they're based on **strong**, with a strong –g.

Stroganoff

This dish, consisting of thinly sliced meats cooked in a sauce of consommé, sour cream, mustard, onion, and spices, is named after Count Paul Stroganoff, a 19th-century Russian diplomat.

stucco

study, studying

stupefy

Only four verbs end in –efy; all the rest end in –ify. The other three are **liquefy, putrefy,** and **rarefy. Stupefy** is from a Latin word meaning "to be stunned."

stymie, stymied

The experts are **stymied** in their efforts to ascertain the origin of this word.

suave

This word comes from the Latin for "delightful and sweet."

sublime

When you spell **sublime**, combine *sub* and *lime* for a majestically good time. This word is from the Latin meaning "uplifted."

submarine

submission

Here's a way of remembering how to spell this word correctly: "Although afraid of the small spaces in a submarine, the sailor submitted to going on a *sub mission*."

Correct spelling   *Incorrect spelling*

submissive
submit, submitted, submitting
To spell these words correctly, double the last consonant before adding the suffixes *–ed* and *–ing* because the accent is on the last syllable of the base word **submit**.

subpoena
This word comes straight from the Latin, meaning "under penalty."

subsequent
subterfuge
This deceptive stratagem comes from a Latin word for "secretly" and the word "flight" as in **fugitive**.

subtle, subtlety, subtly
Subtle comes from the Latin meaning "fine spun" and it can mean delicately woven or difficult to detect. Spell it correctly by remembering that the *–b* in **subtle** is so subtle that it's not pronounced.

succeed
Only three verbs in English end in *–ceed*. (The other two are **exceed** and **proceed**.)

success, succession
Remember that a *–cc* and a *–ss* ensure **success** when spelling these words.

successful, successfully
succulence, succulent
These words are from the Latin, meaning "juice."

sudenim, sudenym   **pseudonym***

suicide
This word is related to the same Latin verb, *cadere* (to cut), as are the other "death" nouns—**homicide, genocide, regicide, pesticide, insecticide, herbicide,** and so forth—and the adjectives **precise** and **concise**.

suite/sweet
These homophones might make you bitter if you spell them incorrectly. A **suite** is a group of furniture or a group of adjoining rooms. **Sweet** is something sugary or cloying.

| **Correct spelling** | *Incorrect spelling* |

sumptuous
This word is from the Latin, meaning "expense."

superb
Add a –*b* to *super* for a word that means outstanding or marvelous. The Latin root, *superbus*, meant "proud," from the word *super* (over, above).

supercede   **supersede***

supercilious
This word for "haughty" or "scornful" derived from a Latin word meaning "eyebrow" and "pride."

superfluity, superfluous
These words come from a Latin verb meaning "to overflow."

superintendent
You get an "A" if you remember there isn't one in this word. Combine the four words *super, in, ten,* and *dent*. The word comes from the Latin verb meaning to "direct one's attention to."

supersede
This is the only verb ending in this sound that's spelled –*sede*. The others are all spelled –*cede* or, in a few cases, –*ceed*. This verb means to take the place of someone or something else, from the Latin verb meaning "to sit above or upon."

supervise
Supervise is one of 11 commonly misspelled words ending in –*ise*. The others are **advertise, advise, apprise, chastise, despise, devise, exercise, improvise, revise,** and **surprise**.

supplement
This word is from the Latin, meaning "complete." A female friend likes this mnemonic device to help her remember how to spell the word correctly: "Many women would like *supple men* to help them around the house."

suppose, supposition

suprise   **surprise***

sureal   **surreal***

surealism   **surrealism***

| **Correct spelling** | *Incorrect spelling* |

surealistic   **surrealistic***
sureptitious   **surreptitious***

surliness, surly

Surly comes from the Middle English meaning "masterful." It later meant "domineering" or "arrogant" and now has shifted meanings to "gruff" and "ill-humored."

surloin   **sirloin**

surmise

This word evolved from a Middle English word meaning "accuse"—perhaps without conclusive proof. From there it's a logical step to the current meaning, "to infer without evidence."

surogate   **surrogate**

surprise

Surprise is one of 11 commonly misspelled words ending in *–ise*. The others are **advertise, advise, apprise, chastise, despise, devise, exercise, improvise, revise,** and **supervise.**

surreal, surrealistic, surrealism

These words come from a French literary movement, from combining *sur* (above or beyond) and *realisme* (realism).

surreptitious

This word, from the Latin meaning, "to seize secretly," refers to an action using clandestine means.

surveillance

Here's a mnemonic to help you spell this word: "The woman under **surveillance** hid her face behind a *veil* to prevent from being seen." This word means to keep a close watch on someone or something by spying.

survival, survive, survivor

susceptibility, susceptible

suspense

Besides **suspense**, only a few words in American English end in *–ense*: **dense, defense, expense, immense, intense, offense, pretense, sense,** and **tense.** The word comes from the same Old French as **suspend**, since **suspense** keeps us hanging.

| **Correct spelling** | *Incorrect spelling* |

suspicion

Suspicion is one of three nouns that end in *–cion*. The others are **coercion** and **scion**. All the rest with the *shun* sound end in *–cian*.

suttle **subtle***

svelte

This word comes through French and Italian from the Latin meaning, "to pull out." The meaning developed into "stretched out"—as in tall, slender, and graceful.

swank, swanky

swave **suave***

sweet/suite (see entry for **suite/sweet**)

sword

sycophant

For the Greeks, a **sycophant** was an informer. The meaning has shifted slightly to mean a fawning flatterer of people of higher rank, position, or wealth in hopes of earning favor.

syllable

This word is from Greek for "combined in pronunciation."

symbiosis, symbiotic

These words come from Greek, meaning "living together."

symbol

symmetrical, symmetry

In these words we recognize the Greek prefix *sym-* (together) and *metron* (measure), a root that we find in such words as **meter**. Remembering these two parts means that you'll remember the double *–mm-*.

sympathetic, sympathy

These words come from the Greek for "feeling together" or "of like emotion."

symphony

symposium

This impressive word generally used for academic or business gatherings comes straight from a Greek word for "drinking party." Some things never change!

| **Correct spelling** | *Incorrect spelling* |

symptom

synagogue

Synagogue comes from Greek, meaning "to bring together," an appropriate origin for a Jewish house of worship.

sync, synch

These are informal words for **synchronization**.

synchronicity, synchronize, synchronous

The Greek word *synchronos*, meaning "same time," gives us these words.

synergism, synergistic, synergy

In these words we find the Greek *syn-* (together) combined with the word for "work," which we also find in **energy**, **ergonomics**, and **ergometric**.

synthesis, synthesize, synthetic

These words come from Greek, meaning "to put together." They are the opposite of **analysis** and **analytical**, which come from the Greek word for "to undo."

syphilis

syringe

Syringe has an interesting origin in the Greek word for "shepherd's pipe," which was made from the hollow stems of the *syringa*, the mock orange shrub.

syrup

This word came into Middle English from Old French, derived from Latin, but the origin is an Arabic verb meaning "to drink." Through the centuries a beverage became a sticky, sweet topping. A variant spelling is **sirup**.

system, systematic, systemic

These words come from Greek, meaning "to set together" or "combine."

tabacco   **tobacco***

tabulate, tabulation

These words come from the Latin *tabula* (writing board)—a word that also gives us **table** and **tablet**.

tacet/tacit

These words come from the same root, which tends to confuse the spelling. **Tacet** is a form of a Latin verb meaning "(it) is silent" and is used as a direction in music to indicate that an instrument is not to play. **Tacit** comes into English through French from the same Latin verb and means "expressed or carried on without words or speech" or "implied or indicated but not actually expressed." You can remember the difference if you think of the e in **tacet** as easy for the musician and that **tacit** ends with the same syllable as its synonym, **implic***it*.

tacit/tacet (see entry for **tacet/tacit**)

tack/tact

These words are not true homophones, but they could nail you with a misspelling. A **tack** is a short nail with a sharp point and a flat head. **Tact** comes from a Latin word meaning "to touch," as in being sensitive.

tact/tack (see entry for **tack/tact**)

tambourine

This word comes from Old French, *tambourin* and *tambour*. Those two words, both meaning "small drum," are also used in English in more restricted ways.

tangent, tangential

These words come from a Latin verb form meaning "touching," but we stop here, to keep from going off on a **tangent**....

Correct spelling   *Incorrect spelling*

tangerine

This fruit was once called a "kid glove orange" because of its ease in peeling. It was possibly grown in Asia, but we acquired it through the port of Tangiers in Morocco—which gives us its name. To help you spell it correctly, remember that the word *anger* is in the middle of **tangerine**.

tantalize

This word derives from a mythological Greek king who was condemned in Hades to stand in a pool of water under a tree branch full of fruit. Every time he attempted to get either, the water level sank or the branch moved away.

tarable   **terrible**

tariff

We get this word through Italian from an Arabic word meaning "notification." It might help with spelling to think of the final *–ff* as standing for "*f*ederal *f*ee."

tarrable   **terrible**

tarriff   **tariff***

tartar

tattoo

This skin art comes from Tahiti, where the word meant "pricking."

taupe

This French word for "mole" rhymes with "hope" and is a brownish-gray color.

tawdry

This word is a contraction of *St. Audrey* (Saint Etheldeda, who was queen of Northumbria). St. Audrey died of a throat tumor that she believed was a punishment for wearing heavy gold necklaces in her youth.

teammate

Join *team* and *mate* to get this word. The *–mm-* remains because the first word ends in the same letter with which the second word begins.

Correct spelling   *Incorrect spelling*

technical, technician, technique
   The Greek root *techne* meant "skill" or "art" and referred to a
   carpenter or weaver skillful at putting things together.

technology, technological
   These words also come from the Greek *techne* (skill) and *–ology*
   (science).

technophobe, technophobia

tedious, tedium
   These words come from the Latin meaning "weariness."

tekila   **tequila***

telecommunicate, telecommunications

telecommute, telecommuter

telepathic, telepathy
   The prefix *tele-* is Greek meaning "from far off" or "at a distance,"
   a root also found in **telephone** and **television**. The second part
   of these words comes from the Greek word for "suffering" and,
   by extension, "feeling."

temperament, temperamental
   These words come from the Latin as applied to the medieval
   physiology of the humors, and the balance of hot, cold, moist, and
   dry.

temperance
   This word comes from the Latin meaning "to mix in the proper
   proportions."

temperarily   **temporarily**

temperary   **temporary**

temperature

temperment   **temperament***

tempermental   **temperamental***

tempo
   This musical word comes to English through Italian from the Latin
   for "time."

temporary, temporarily

| **Correct spelling** | *Incorrect spelling* |

temprature	**temperature**

tenacious, tenacity
We get these words from the Latin meaning "to hold fast."

tenament	**tenement***

tenancy
Tenancy is the property held by a **tenant**.

tenant/tenet
These words are not true homophones and you won't be evicted if you misspell them. A **tenant** is someone who lives in a residence, but doesn't own it. A **tenet** is a belief to hold on to (from the Latin "to hold fast.")

tenative	**tentative**

tendency
This word comes from the Latin "to touch" or "to try," hence the meaning of experimental or uncertain.

tendinitis

tendon

tendonitis	**tendinitis**

tenement
You can spell this word with ease if you remember to spell it with only e's (three of them).

tenent	**tenant***

tenet/tenant (see entry for **tenant/tenet**)

tennative	**tentative**
tennent	**tenant***

tense
Besides **tense**, only a few words in American English end in –*ense*: **dense, defense, expense, immense, intense, offense, pretense, sense,** and **suspense**.

tentative

tenuous

tenure
This word comes from the Latin meaning "to hold" and represents a period during which something is held.

Correct spelling	*Incorrect spelling*

tequila

This word comes from the plant that's the source of the drink, *agave tequilana*. The plant was named after a district in Mexico.

terace	**terrace**
teradactyl	**pterodactyl***
terafy	**terrify**
terasse	**terrace**
tererism	**terrorism**
terible	**terrible**
teridactyl	**pterodactyl***
terific	**terrific***
terify	**terrify**

terminal

This word comes from the Latin *terminus*, meaning "boundary" or "limit," a word that we use in English for the end of certain things. The root also evolved into **terminate** and **term**.

termoil	**turmoil**
ternament	**tournament***
terodactyl	**pterodactyl***
teror	**terror**
terorism	**terrorism**

terrace

terradactyl	**pterodactyl***
terrafy	**terrify**

terra incognita

This phrase is pure Latin for "unfamiliar ground."

terrasse	**terrace**
terrerism	**terrorism**

terrible

terridactyl	**pterodactyl***

terrific

This word comes from the same Latin root as **terrify**, but down

Correct spelling	*Incorrect spelling*

through the centuries the meaning of **terrific** has changed drastically from something **terrible** that causes **terror**.

terrify

terrodactyl   **pterodactyl***

terrorism

testacle   **testicle**

testament

testamony   **testimony**

testicle

testiment   **testament**

testimony

than/then

Confusion is easy with these two words. **Than** introduces the second part of a comparison of greater or lesser. **Then** means a specific time.

theef   **thief**

theeve   **thieve**

theif   **thief**

their/there/they're

These homophones often cause great confusion. **Their** is the possessive case of the pronoun "they." **There** means at that place, as opposed to here. **They're** is a contraction for "they are."

theive   **thieve**

then/than (see entry for **than/then**)

there/they're/their (see entry for **their/there/they're**)

thermal

thermometer

This word is formed from the Greek words for "hot" and "measure."

they're/there/their (see entry for **their/there/they're**)

thief, thieve, thieves

Correct spelling   *Incorrect spelling*

thingamajig

thorofare **thoroughfare***

thorough
> This mnemonic might prevent a misspelled word: "It can be *rough* to spell **tho*rough*** correctly."

thoroughfare
> The **thorough** in this English word originally meant **through**.

threshold

threw/through
> Don't let these homophones throw you. **Threw** is the past tense of **throw**. **Through** means "finished."

through/threw (see entry for **threw/through**)

tic/tick
> Don't go into spasms over these homophones. A **tic** is an involuntary spasm, while a **tick** can be the sound made by a clock or watch, a mark used to check off something, a bloodsucking arachnid, or a mattress cover.

tick/tic (see entry for **tic/tick**)

tinge, tingeing
> **Tinge** is one of two verbs that end in –e that keep the e when adding –*ing*. The other verb is **singe**, which becomes **singeing**.

tipe **type***

tipical **typical***

tipo **typo***

tipoes **typos***

tiranical **tyrannical***

tiranous **tyrannous***

tirant **tyrant***

tirany **tyranny***

titillate, titillation
> You'll find the word *till* in the middle of these words that come from the Latin meaning "to tickle."

Correct spelling *Incorrect spelling*

to/too/two
These homophones can be quite challenging. **To** is a preposition, **too** means "also," and **two** is the number after one.

tobacco
This Spanish word comes from a West Indies word for a pipe in which the natives smoked the leaves of the tobacco plant.

together

tomain, tomane   **ptomaine***

tomato, tomatoes
This word comes to us through the Spanish from a language used by Indians in Mexico and Central America. The fruit was initially thought to be harmful, but the French thought it was an aphro-disiac and referred to it as the "love apple."

tomorrow

tongue
The *–ngue* ending occurs only in the words **tongue, harangue,** and **meringue,** all words from the French.

tonight

too/to/two (see entry for **to/too/two**)

tope   **taupe***

tornado, tornadoes
This Spanish word originally meant a thunderstorm—somewhat of an understatement.

tortilla

total, totaled (or totalled), totaling (or totalling), totally

totalitarian

tough

tournament
Here's a mnemonic to help with this one: **tournament** contains the words *tour* and *name.*

toxic, toxicity
These words are derived from the Latin word for "poison," which came from the Greek word for a "bow" and referred to one using arrows dipped in poison.

Correct spelling   *Incorrect spelling*

track/tract

Although these aren't quite homophones, they are similar enough to throw you off the path. A **track** is a path along which something moves. A **tract** is a limited area of land.

tract/track (see entry for **track/tract**)

tradgedy   **tragedy***

traffic

trafficked, trafficking

When we add *–ed* or *–ing* to **traffic**, we insert a *–k* to keep the final *–c* hard. We do the same with other verbs ending in *–c*, such as **panic** and **picnic**: **panicked** and **panicking**, and **picnicked** and **picnicking**.

trafic   **traffic**

traficed   **trafficked***

traficing   **trafficking***

tragedy, tragic

To spell this word correctly, remember that the word *rage* is at the center of **tragedy.** The Greek root word was a combination of the words for "goat" and "song"—humble beginnings for the theatrical tradition of the Western world.

traitor

To spell this word correctly, combine *trait* and *or*.

trama   **trauma**

transcendent, transcendental, transcendentalism

These words come from the Latin, meaning "to climb beyond."

transfer, transferring, transference

transgress, transgression

In these words we recognize the prefix *trans-*, as in **transfer** and **transmit**, and the root *–gress* and *–gression*, as in **progress** and **progression** or **regress** and **regression**.

trater   **traitor***

trauma

| **Correct spelling** | *Incorrect spelling* |

trayter	**traitor***

treacherous, treachery

tread

treck	**trek***
tred	**tread**

trek

This word might have faded from use if not for a TV series and a string of movies that featured it in their titles. The word is a rare borrowing straight from Afrikaans, where it meant "to travel by ox wagon," from the Dutch verb, *trekken* (to travel).

trellis

trespass

trist	**tryst***

triumvirate

trough

Use this mnemonic to help you spell this word: "The golfer put the ball on the **t**ee and hit it into the *rough*."

true, truly

Truly is an exception to the rule when adding the suffix –*ly* to a word that ends in a silent –*e*. With **truly,** you drop the silent –*e* before adding the suffix.

tryst

You won't misspell this word if you remember that the lovers decided to *try* a new meeting place. The originally meaning of the word **tryst**—an appointed hunting station where a hunter lay in wait for his prey—was not at all romantic.

tube, tubular

Tuesday

This day of the week was named after the Germanic god of war. It was *Tiwesday* in Middle English, so at least it's gotten a little easier to spell over the last few centuries!

tuff	**tough**

Correct spelling   *Incorrect spelling*

tumor

tumult, tumultuous
These words come from the Latin for "swelling" as in **tumor**, but with a more specific use, as in swelling of sound.

tunge **tongue***

turmoil

turnament **tournament***

twirl
This word was formed by combining the words **twist** and **whirl**.

two/to/too (see entry for **to/too/two**)

type, typical
These words come from a Greek word meaning "impression," a root that we also find in printing **type** and **typewriter**.

typo, typos
A **typo** was originally printing trade slang for "typographical error." Then, **typo** extended to the typewriter. Now we can make a **typo** on a keyboard as well. Progress! There's no —e in the plural.

tyrannical, tyrannous, tyranny, tyrant
These words come from the Greek for "absolute ruler who governs without laws or restrictions." The root was also used to name the **tyrannosaurus**.

ubiquitous, ubiquity

The Latin root, *ubique*, means "everywhere." To help spell these words correctly, remember that the word *quit* is in the middle of them.

Incorrect spelling	Correct spelling
ucalale	**ukulele***
ucalyptus	**eucalyptus**
ufemism	**euphemism***
ufemistic	**euphemistic***
ufemistically	**euphemistically***
uforia	**euphoria**
uforic	**euphoric**
ugenics	**eugenics***

ukulele

This word comes from the Hawaiian for "jumping flea." This instrument was modified from a Portuguese guitar.

Incorrect spelling	Correct spelling
ulagize	**eulogize***
ulagy	**eulogy***

ulcer, ulcerous

Incorrect spelling	Correct spelling
ulogize	**eulogize***
ulogy	**eulogy***

ulterior

This word is pure Latin, meaning "more remote" or "more on the other side." It's related to **ultimate**, **ultimatum**, and the prefix **ultra**.

ultimate

Correct spelling   *Incorrect spelling*

ultimatum

ultruistic   **altruistic**

umbrage

This word for "offense" comes from the Latin word for "shadow," which is also the root of the more common word, **umbrella**. An **umbrella** was originally to provide shade from the sun, as in **parasol**, rather than protection from rain.

unanimity, unanimous

The *un-* in these words doesn't indicate an opposite; it's a form of the Latin word for "one," as in **union**. The main part of these words comes from *animus*, "mind."

uncanny

uncommitted

To spell this word correctly, double the final consonant before adding a suffix because the accent is on the final syllable of the root word, **commit**.

uncommon

unconscionable

uncouth

This word has its roots in Old English, meaning "unknown" or "strange."

unctuous

This word comes from the Latin word *unguentum*. This root also gives us **unguent** and **ointment**. An **unctuous** person is insincere and as slippery as **ointment**.

under way

This expression should be spelled as two words, with the rare exception of ships that are in motion—then it's **underway**.

undoubtedly

The root, **doubt**, comes from the Latin verb *dubitare* (to waver), a word that we also find in **indubitably,** a fancy synonym for **undoubtedly**.

unequivocal

Correct spelling   *Incorrect spelling*

unic	**eunuch*, unique***

union

unique

This word is pure French, from a Latin word for "sole" or "only."

unkanny	**uncanny**

unnecessarily, unnecessary

unparalleled

unruly

until

This is a Middle English word. Oddly, the *un-* doesn't indicate a negative; it also meant "till," which is why **until** and **till** are exact synonyms.

unuch	**eunuch***

updateable

uphemism	**euphemism***
uphemistic	**euphemistic***
uphemistically	**euphemistically***

upholster, upholstery

The root of these words is Middle English and meant "to repair" in a generic sense. It might help in spelling to remember **upholster** as consisting of the two words **up** and **holster**.

uphoria	**euphoria**
uphoric	**euphoric**

urban/urbane

Although not true homophones, these words often get confused. **Urban** means "characteristic of a city," while **urbane** means "sophisticated, elegant, and refined." Both of these words are from the Latin *urbanus*, "pertaining to a city," but **urbane** came through French.

urbane/urban (see entry for **urban/urbane**)

urchin

This word originally meant "hedgehog"—an origin that makes sense if we consider the sea urchin rather than a scruffy child.

Correct spelling	*Incorrect spelling*

urve   **oeuvre**

This word is used in English in the expression **hors d'oeuvre** and in referring to an artist's body of work. The word is pure French, for "work."

usual, usually

usurious, usury

These words for exorbitant interest on loans come from Latin, based on the word for "use."

utensil

This word came from the Latin root, *utensilis*, which meant "fit for use," from the root that we find in such words as **utility**, **utilize**, and **utilitarian**.

uterus

uthanasia   **euthanasia***

utopia

This word is from the Greek meaning "not a place." Sir Thomas More used it to describe an imaginary island. The more recent definition is an ideally perfect place or condition.

uturus   **uterus**

Correct spelling   *Incorrect spelling*

vacancy, vacant

vacation/vocation

Don't confuse these words in your leisure. **Vacation** is a period of rest from work from the Latin verb *vacare* (to be empty or at leisure). **Vocation** is a regular occupation or calling, from the Latin verb *vocare* (to call).

vacillate, vacillation

vaccinate, vaccine

A **vaccine** is a preventive medicine administered in doses measured in "ccs." These words come from the Latin word for "cow," *vacca*. The disease of smallpox was eradicated by taking a virus from cows, cowpox, and injecting it into humans as a **vaccine**. To prevent the disease of a misspelled word, **vaccinate** yourself with a dose of two –ccs.

vaccum	**vacuum***
vaccuous	**vacuous**
vaccuum	**vacuum***
vacsinate	**vaccinate***
vacsine	**vaccine***

vacuous

vacuum

This word comes from the same Latin verb as **vacation**—*vacare* (to be empty). Remember the double –*uu*—for the original "s**u**ck-**u**p."

vagabond

This word is from a Latin word meaning "wandering," and original-ly referred to an itinerant rogue, loafer, or vagrant. Now it has a

Correct spelling	*Incorrect spelling*

much more romantic meaning. **Vagabond** is related to the **vague** and **vagary**.

vagary, vagaries

vague

vail **vale/veil***

vain/vane/vein

> **Vain** means "unsuccessful" or "conceited." **Vane** is a device that shows the direction of the wind. What confuses some people is that the noun form of **vain** is **vanity**. The root is the Latin *vanus*, "empty." **Vein** comes from the old French, *veine*, which comes from Latin, *veña*, meaning blood vessel.

vakume **vacuum***

valadate **validate***

valadation **validation***

vale/veil

> A **vale** is "a valley, a dale." **Veil** is a piece of cloth or netting or "to cover, conceal, or disguise." (There's also **Vail**, a resort town in Colorado.)

valet

valey **valley**

validate, validation, validity

> These three words evolved from the Latin *validus*, "strong," from a verb that also developed into such words as **valiant, valence, valor,** and **valedictorian**.

vallet **valet**

valley

valt **vault**

valuable, value, valued, valuing

vandal

> Yesterday's **Vandals** were a Germanic tribe that overran Gaul and sacked Rome. (When in Rome, undo what the Romans do?) Today's **vandals** destroy property a little closer to home.

vane/vain/vein (see entry for **vain/vane/vein**)

Correct spelling	*Incorrect spelling*

vanereal   **venereal***

vanguard

We also use the Old French root of **vanguard** in a synonym—
avant-garde.

vanilla

The word for this spice comes from the Spanish for "little sheath,"
so named because of the shape of the seed pods.

vanity

vanquish

varied, variety, various, vary, varied

vascilate   **vacillate**

vascilation   **vacillation**

vasectomy

vault

vegetable

Here's a mnemonic to help you spell this word correctly: "The
vitamins in a **vegetable** help you *get able* to stay healthy."

vegetarian

vehicle

vehicular

vehicule   **vehicle**

veil/vale (see entry for **vale/veil**)

vein/vain/vane (see entry for **vain/vane/vein**)

venereal

This word, generally used only in the term "**venereal** disease,"
which has been replaced by the more clinical "sexually transmitted
disease," is an adjective derived from Latin, from a form of **Venus**.

vengeance

This word for revenge comes through French from the Latin verb,
vindicare (to avenge), which also appears in **vindicate** and **vindictive**.

ventilate

Correct spelling	*Incorrect spelling*

A suggested mnemonic: "To prevent suffocation, combine *vent* and *i* and *late*."

veracity

verbal, verbalize

verbatim
This word is pure Latin for "in exactly the same words."

verbose, verbosity

verge

vernal
This word describes the **equinox** (Latin for "equal night") appropriate to spring.

verses/versus
Verses is the plural of **verse**, a line or unit of poetry or song.
Versus means "against," often abbreviated as "v." or "vs."

versus/verses (see entry for **verses/versus**)

vertical
This word comes from the Latin, *vertex*, meaning highest point and, by extension, any line going up toward a highest point.

vertigo

vetanarian	**veterinarian***
vetanary	**veterinary***

veteran

veteranarian	**veterinarian***
veteranary	**veterinary***
veteren	**veteran**

veterinarian, veterinary
These words derived from the Latin word for "beasts of burden."

vibe
This word is a shortened form of **vibration** and means an instinctive feeling about a person or thing.

vicarious

vice versa

Correct spelling	*Incorrect spelling*

This expression is pure Latin, meaning "the position being reversed."

vichyssoise
The root word of this cold potato soup flavored with leeks is *Vichy,* a town in France that was named the capital of the country during World War II.

vicinity

vicious, viciously
These words are easy to spell if you remember that they come from the same root as **vice.**

vicissitude

vie, vying
Many verbs like **vie,** that end in an *–ie,* change to a *–y* when you add the suffix *–ing.* Three other examples are **die—dying, lie—lying,** and **tie—tying.**

Incorrect spelling	Correct spelling
vigelance	**vigilance***
vigelant	**vigilant***
vigelante	**vigilante***
viger	**vigor***
vigerous	**vigorous***

vigilant, vigilante, vigilance
Combine *vigil* and *ant* and you'll be alert. These words go back to Latin, *vigil,* "on the watch." The form **vigilante** (person belonging to a **vigilance** group) came into English through Spanish.

vignette
This French word originally meant "little vine" or the decorative leafy design that was placed at the beginning and/or end of book chapters or along the edges of the pages. From that it was a small, logical step to using this word to refer to short passages or theatrical scenes.

vigor, vigorous
The Latin root, *vigor,* came from a verb meaning "to be lively."

vijilance	**vigilance***

Correct spelling	*Incorrect spelling*

vijilant	**vigilant***
vijilantee	**vigilante***
vilafy	**vilify***
vilage	**village***
vilager	**villager***
vilain	**villain***
vilainous	**villainous***
vilainy	**villainy***

vilify, vilified, vilification
   The Latin root meant "to make worthless," deriving from *vilis*, "worthless."

village, villager
   Village developed through Middle English and Old French from the Latin *villa*, "country estate."

villain, villainous, villainy
   To spell these words correctly, remember that the second syllable is –*ain*- as in the p*ain* caused by a **villain**. The word **villain** was first used in the feudal system for a serf who was bound to the villa of a lord.

vinager	**vinegar***

vindicate

vindictive

vinegar
   The word for this liquid came from the French for "sour wine," the first and best source of vinegar.

vineyard
   Spell this word correctly by combining *vine* and *yard* to get an expanse of cultivated grapes.

vintage
   This word comes from a Middle English version of an Old French word for "grape harvest."

vinyard	**vineyard***

viola

| **Correct spelling** | *Incorrect spelling* |

This is a musical instrument—and the way that people sometimes incorrectly spell the French borrowing, **voilà** or (anglicized) **voila.**

violate, violation

violence, violent

The Latin root of these words is the same as for **violate,** "to force."

viral

virtual

virtue, virtuous

The concept of **virtue** goes back to the Latin *vir*, which meant "man." This root evolved into such words as **virile, triumvirate,** and **virago**(!).

virus

The word **virus,** borrowed from Latin, originally meant "poison," specifically venom from a snake or a spider. The same root is found in **virulent.**

viscious	**vicious***
visciously	**viciously***

viscosity, viscous

These words pertaining to the thickness of a fluid come from *viscum*, the Latin word for "mistletoe." A sticky substance made from mistletoe was used to capture small birds—the early predecessor of our flypaper. Don't confuse **viscous** with **vicious.**

visinity	**vicinity**

visionary

visious	**vicious***
visiously	**viciously***

visualize

vital, vitality

vitamin

vitriol, vitriolic

These words have their root in the Latin word for glass, *vitrium*,

Correct spelling	*Incorrect spelling*

which also gives us **vitreous**. The development of meaning into our current sense of "scathing" or "vituperative" is interesting, but too involved to relate here.

vivacious, vivacity

vizionary   **visionary**

vizualize   **visualize**

vocation/vacation (see entry for **vacation/vocation**)

vociferous

vogue

voilà

This French word is used to point out something, often a result or an accomplishment. The anglicized variant spelling is without the accent, **voila**.

volume, voluminous

These words are from the Latin for "to turn about" or "roll," a root that evolved into words such as **evolution**. The first **volumes** were rolls of writing.

voracious

This word is from the Latin for "to swallow" or "to devour." That verb is the root of *devorare*, which became **devour**.

vulnerable, vulnerability

The Latin root, *vulnus*, means **wound**.

wanderlust

Combine the words *wander* and *lust* for this direct borrowing from the German, which means "a passion for traveling."

warrant, warranty

Warrant came into Middle English from a Germanic word that also gave us **guarantee**. Remember how to spell **warrant** correctly with this mnemonic: "During the *war* the soldier *ran* from a **warrant** officer."

watchword

watershed

way/weigh/whey

Way is a manner, a method, a course, a direction, or a respect. **Weigh** means "to measure **weight**." **Whey** is the liquid that separates from the curd in coagulated milk.

weak/week

The first of these homophones is a synonym of "feeble" or "poor" and the second is a unit of seven days and nights.

weasel

Spell this word by remembering that to get out of things with *ease* is to **weasel**.

weather/whether

Weather means the state of the atmosphere or to withstand, while **whether** introduces an alternative. To remember the difference, use these mnemonics: "I don't want to *eat* in hot **weather**." And "I don't know **whether** a snack would *whet* my appetite."

weazle   **weasel**

Wednesday

This day of the week was named after the Germanic god Woden,

Correct spelling   *Incorrect spelling*

in the Old English *Wodnesdaeg.* Just remember goo**d** ol**d** go**d** Wo**d**en and you won't likely forget the silent –**d**.

week/weak (see entry for **weak/week**)

weesel   **weasel***

weigh/way/whey (see entry for **way/weigh/whey**)

weird

> One of six exceptions to the "*i* before *e* except after *c*" rule. The others are **either, neither, leisure,** and **seize** and **seizure.** The word **weird** once meant fate or destiny, as in the Weird Sisters (the three fates of mythology). The meaning has changed considerably.

we're/were

> The first of these homophones is a contraction of "we are" and the second is a past tense of the verb "to be."

were/we're (see entry for **we're/were**)

werewolf

> In Old English and Germanic languages, *wer* and its variants meant "man," so a **werewolf** is a man-wolf.

whether/weather (see entry for **weather/whether**)

whey/way/weigh (see entry for **way/weigh/whey**)

which/witch

> **Which** helps identify what one or more of a group. A **witch** is a sorceress.

whim, whimsical

whistful   **wistful**

whistfully   **wistfully**

whistle

whole/hole (see entry for **hole/whole**)

whole, wholly

whore

who's/whose

> **Who's** is a contraction for "who is." **Whose** is a pronoun meaning "that which belongs to whom."

Correct spelling	*Incorrect spelling*

whose/who's (see entry for **who's/whose**)

wierd	**weird***
wimen	**women***
wim	**whim**
wimsical	**whimsical**

wistful, wistfully

wistle	**whistle**

witch/which (see entry for **which/witch**)

withhold

Combine *with* and *hold* for this word that means "to hold away." The –*hh*- is logical, although it may look odd.

women

wonderful

worldwide

worship, worshiped or **worshipped, worshiper, worshiping** or **worshipping**

wrack/rack (see entry for **rack/wrack**)

wrath, wrathful

These words have held the meaning of "anger" and "angry" from their origins in Old English.

wreak/reek (see entry for **reek/wreak**)

wreath

wreckless	**reckless**
wreeth	**wreath**

wring/ring (see entry for **ring/wring**)

write/right/rite (see entry for **right/rite/write**)

writer, writing, written

wrote/rote (see entry for **rote/wrote**)

wunderful	**wonderful**

Correct spelling	*Incorrect spelling*

xenophobe, xenophobia

These words derive from two Greek words: *xenos* for "stranger" and *phobos* for "fear."

Xerox

This is a trademark for copy machines using **xerography** and the name of a company. It should not be used as a generic term for photocopying.

Xmas

Greek Christians used X (chi) to represent Christ, so this shortened version of "Christmas" represents the intent of the season—even though most people prefer the longer form.

xylophone

The name of this instrument, which is composed of parallel wooden bars arranged in a musical scale and struck by small mallets, comes from the Greek words for "wood sound."

Correct spelling   *Incorrect spelling*

yahoo

This term for a crude or brutish person was invented by Jonathan Swift for his imaginary race of brutes in human form. The brutes are found in Swift's fourth book of *Gulliver's Travels*.

year, yearly

yeast

yeild   **yield***

yeoman

yere   **year**

yield

This word is easy to spell correctly if you keep in mind the old rule of "*i* before *e* except after *c*."

yesterday

yoga, yogi

These words are rare borrowings from Sanskrit, where the word transliterated as **yoga** means "union" or "yoking," in reference to the goal of gaining control of body and mind.

yogurt

This word for thick, curdled milk to which bacteria have been added is Turkish.

yoke/yolk

Don't get scrambled up spelling these homophones. **Yoke** is a wooden frame to connect two draft animals, such as horses or oxen, while **yolk** is the yellow portion of an egg.

yolk/yoke (see entry for **yoke/yolk**)

Correct spelling   *Incorrect spelling*

yore/your/you're

Yore is an old word meaning "time long past." **Your** is adjective that indicates that something belongs to you or is being considered in relationship to you. **You're** is a contraction of "you are."

young, youngster

your/yore/you're (see entry for yore/your/you're)

you're/yore/your (see entry for yore/your/you're)

yucca

Yucca is Spanish word of American Indian origin for a large, cactus-like plant.

Correct spelling	Incorrect spelling
yufemism	**euphemism***
yuforia	**euphoria**
yukka	**yucca***
yulogise, yulogize	**eulogize***
yulogy	**eulogy***
yung	**young**
yungster	**youngster**
yunick	**eunuch***
yuthanasia, yuthenasia	**euthanasia***

zeal, zealot, zealous
The word **zeal** goes back to Greek; the root also evolved into **jealousy** and **jealous**. The first zealots were a 1st century Jewish fundamentalist group that used violence and assassination to avoid Roman control.

zebra
The Portuguese word for this African equine mammal means a "disappearing donkey."

zefer	**zephyr***

zeitgeist
The vowel pattern of –*ei* is repeated twice in this German word for "spirit of the times." The second half of this word appears also in **poltergeist**.

zele	**zeal***
zelot	**zealot***
zelous	**zealous***

zenith
This word comes from an Arabic word meaning a path (over the head) in the sky.

zenophobe	**xenophobe***
zenophobia	**xenophobia***

zephyr
The Greeks called the West wind, the mildest of the four winds, a **zephyr**.

zercon	**zircon***

zero
We get this word for nothing from Italian, which borrowed it

Correct spelling   *Incorrect spelling*

from Arabic, the language of the people who invented this concept. The original word, transliterated as *sifr*, passed through Latin,
Old French, and Middle English to become **cipher**, which was
originally another word for **zero**.

Zeus

In Greek mythology, Zeus was the supreme deity and the father
of all the other gods and mortal heroes. (His Roman counterpart
was Jupiter.)

zilaphone   **xylophone***

zinnia

This flower, which is native to Mexico and the Southwest, was
named after an 18th-century German botanist, J.G. Zinn.

zircon

This word for "colored gemstone" originated in Italian, passed
into French and German, and then eventually into English.

zitegiste   **zeitgeist***

zodiac

This word comes from the Greek *zoion*, which means "circle of little living beings." That root also developed into words such as
zoology. The ancient Greeks thought that an imaginary belt of 12
animals encircled the heavens.

zoology, zoological

These words are easy to spell if you just start with **zoo**, which is
short for "**zoological** garden."

zucchini

Remember to put a –cc in the middle of this Italian word that
means "little gourds." (A friend who's only too familiar with the
profusion of these vegetables from her garden suggests that the
–cc- stands for "**c**opious **c**onsumption.") The –h- is required in
Italian to keep the c's hard preceding the *i*.

Zues   **Zeus***

zukini   **zucchini***

zylophone   **xylophone***

| **Correct spelling** | *Incorrect spelling* |